London Diaries

by Lorenza Mazzetti

to Lindsay Anderson

Oh Captain!

My Captain!

*This book is dedicated to William Coldstream,
Dennis Forman and Lindsay Anderson*

*I thank Clare and Bernardo Bertolucci for giving
me the English translation of this book. They are
helping me just as Attilio Bertolucci and Zavattini
did for my first book.*

Translated from the Italian by Melinda Mele
All images reproduced courtesy of Lorenza Mazzetti
First published in English by Zidane Press in 2018,
Copyright@ Zidane Press Ltd.
ISBN: 978-0956267856

Original copyright Sellerio Publishing, Palermo.
Design and layout by Hannah Rae Alton

Cover image: Guillaume Chapaltine, Lindsay Anderson,
Lorenza Mazzetti and Richard Harris in Rome on the terrace
of the house of Via Vittoria 10. Photograph by Bruno
Grieco.

Distributed by:
Turnaround Publisher Services Ltd,
Unit 3, Olympia Trading Estate,
London, N22 6TZ
T. +44 (0)206 829 3019

www.zidanepress.org.uk
British Library Cataloguing in Publication data.
A catalogue record for this book is available from the British
Library.

＊

At the start of the 1950s, Lorenza Mazzetti, an
Italian woman in her twenties, came on her own to
London in order to escape her traumatic past. A
self-confessed outsider, Mazzetti would become a
female pioneer at the heart of Britain's burgeoning
anti-establishment culture. Mazzetti, is a
mesmerising storyteller, both in person, and in
the films, novels and paintings with which she has
recorded her life. Her London Diary provides a
first hand account of the significant cultural shifts
of 1950s London and gives a unique insight into
her part in the founding of the influential Free
Cinema movement. Leading British artists and
filmmakers including Michael Andrews, Eduardo
Paolozzi, William Coldstream, Lindsay
Anderson, Karel Reisz and Tony Richardson all
feature, alongside the diverse and extraordinary

'ordinary' citizens of London. All are observed by what Mazzetti terms her 'right eye, the eye of truth'.

Lorenza and her twin sister Paola were born in 1928 in Florence. Orphaned at a young age, they were sent to live with an aunt, a Jewish uncle and cousins. These relatively happy times ended in 1944, when Nazi soldiers murdered their aunt and their two young cousins, in the Strage di Rignano massacre. Lorenza and Paola were spared due to their different family name, but in 1945 their uncle committed suicide, unable to cope with his grief. Lorenza Mazzetti's life and works explore the struggles to reclaim her identity after the trauma of her early life.

In London Diary, Mazzetti's vulnerability as an unaccompanied woman in 1950's London is particularly striking, and Mazzetti propels her way through assaults, love affairs, itinerant jobs, London landladies, and kind English 'bobbies'. Professor William Coldstream, head of the Slade School of Fine Art, was one of the many individuals who, on encountering Mazzetti, was charmed into ignoring normal protocols, and offered her a place to study. The art school environment provided her with a sanctuary of freedom, friendship and possibilities. It was Coldstream who enlisted the head of the British Film Institute, Denis Forman, to see Mazzetti's first short film 'K' (1954), made when she was a Slade student. This led to the British Film Institute's Experimental Film Fund financing 'Together' (1956). Filmed amongst the now almost vanished communities of the East End of London with its markets, streets, industry, pubs, bomb-sites and gangs of children, 'Together' entangles the emotional state of its director with the environment and sounds of the East End and the cut-off isolation of the two 'deaf-mutes' featured in the film.

London Diary provides a detailed account of the production of 'Together', plus Mazzetti's subsequent role in the Free Cinema movement, its manifesto and its dissemination of experimental films to an audience eager for change. It was Mazzetti's initiative and films that acted as a catalyst for the Slade School of Fine Art to open Britain's first university film department in 1960, under the pioneering film director Thorold Dickinson.

Mazzetti's seminal films 'K' and 'Together' were followed in 1961 by her novel 'Il cielo cade' (The Sky Falls) published in 1961, a compelling account of the war and the Strage di Rignano massacre from the perspective of a child. Other novels followed, and in 2014, Lorenza Mazzetti's account of her time in London was published in Italian.

London Diary reminds us that the young artists, filmmakers and writers of 1950's London were sensitive to the value of London's social, cultural and ethnic diversity. Somehow, genuine experimentation and radical mavericks were able to build a cultural history whose impact and legacy continued far beyond its original context. Lorenza Mazzetti, with her distinctive wit and sensibility, occupies a significant place within that history.

Brighid Lowe

Brighid Lowe is an artist and Senior Lecturer at the Slade School of Fine Art, University College London. She has been researching Lorenza Mazzetti and the history of the Slade Film Department.

I

I wanted to run away from Tuscany, from Florence, and from that beautiful house with windows overlooking the Arno River and with a view of San Miniato. Their dresses are still hanging in the closets, the clothes that belong to our aunt and uncle - our adoptive parents - and to our two little cousins Luce and Cicci. They are all resting in the churchyard of the Badiuzza in San Donato in Collina. Only my twin sister Baby and I are left in the big house on Lungarno delle Grazie.

I asked my guardian to give me money to go to England, where I would spend the holidays on a farm getting paid for my work.

I leave with a group of philosophy students, on a trip organised by the University of Florence where I've just enrolled, which offers a stipend to the students who go to work on an English farm.

I can't wait to sail on the ship across the English Channel and see the famous White Cliffs of Dover, but my hopes for a wonderful crossing fade as I spend hours vomiting in the company of other seasick passengers.

When I arrive in England the first police officers I meet ask for my passport, and to my surprise search me from head to toe while mumbling to each other. I'm ordered to open my rucksack and my suitcase. After a long while, they return my passport with a stamp. I thank them and finally enter England. Looking at my passport, I'm shocked to read on the stamp the words "Undesirable Alien".

At last I arrive at the farm, not far from London. I'm so excited!

For the first time in my life I eat cornflakes with milk and sugar. It seems so wonderful that I'm beside myself with joy. The countryside is beautiful, but so different from the Tuscan landscapes I'm used to.

All of us students are ready to work. We're asked to carry sacks full of potatoes from one place to another. I see the others take the heavy burden on their backs and still manage to move forward to their destination.

It's my turn. A sack of potatoes is placed on my shoulders and I find myself on the ground, flattened under an enormous weight. I'm dumbfounded.

The English boss is very annoyed. He realises I'm useless at that task and takes me to another site, where the potatoes run on a conveyor belt. You have to leave the good ones and discard the bad ones. And you have to do it very quickly, because the potatoes run by very fast.

The boss watches me to see if I'm good at it, so I become self-conscious and get confused. I throw away the good ones and leave the bad ones. He notices, yanks my arm and once again takes me away.

He's convinced I'm doing it on purpose, but luckily it's lunchtime. Instead of allowing me to eat, however, the boss has me stir a large pot of rice that's cooking for the students' meal. As the water evaporates, the rice becomes harder and harder to stir. I start screaming because I can't take it anymore. He thinks I'm faking it and doesn't come to help, and the rice burns. I ruined everyone's lunch.

The next day the boss puts me in the cowshed to turn over manure. It's an exhausting task because the manure is very hard, and after an hour he thinks I've done too little.

He drags me to my tent and tells me to pack my suitcase and leave. He escorts me to the exit and leaves me by the side of the road, telling me to hitchhike to the city and find myself another job. I call Baby and describe my misadventures to her, telling her I'm waiting for the guardian to send me money.

II

While waiting for the money to arrive, I find a room in a small boarding house. I go around visiting museums. In the meantime, I pay for the room with all the money I had left. The London museums are stunning.

After a few days I ring Baby to let her know the money hasn't arrived. Her boyfriend answers the phone. He is cross and tells me that I shouldn't call all the time and that twins ought to learn to live separately. Baby says that she's sure the guardian would be sending me money.

London was so different from our cities that I finally feel like I'm elsewhere.

After a month the money still hasn't arrived.

I ring Baby and she tells me that certainly it will be coming. Baby tries to console me, but in the background I can hear Stephen calling her and telling her not to spend so much time on the phone.

I stay on the phone with her for an hour and I burst out crying.

I walk out of the phone booth.

It's cold and dark.

"May I escort you, Miss? Aren't you afraid to be out at this hour by yourself?"

I wonder why young women who walk around on their own always have to be persecuted by some fellow.

"No," I answer, "I'd rather walk alone."

"Why, why?"

"Because I prefer it, thank you."

"Why do you prefer it? Am I bothering you?"

"No, it's not that you're bothering me, in fact you're very kind, but I'd rather walk by myself."

"Well then, I'll leave you alone."

"Thank you."

"I hope that I haven't offended you."

"Of course not, why would you have offended me?"

"In that case, if I haven't offended you Miss, let's shake hands, make peace and leave as good friends."

"But we haven't argued."

"No, but after all I did bother you and I'm sorry. Give me your hand and let's make peace. If you'll give me your hand, I won't follow you anymore."

I gave him my hand and he never gave it back.

He stuck his tongue inside my mouth, sucking my lips until they hurt. As he pressed me against a wall, his tongue roaming ferociously and feverishly between my lips. I was startled and stunned and could barely breathe, and managed to disengage. But his tongue, penetrating boldly and furiously, had smothered my mouth, stealing pieces of my soul. My abducted hand was dragged along a corridor between our bodies, through a door to his pants that had magically opened... leading who knows where.

No longer belonging to me, my hand became a delicate instrument in the hands of a stranger. My tongue had been stolen and was now between the teeth of the stranger as if that was where it naturally belonged.

He was pressing me so hard against the building that my shoulder blades became one with the stone. One breast was no longer mine. The thief fondled it as if it were ivory to be buffed and polished. He would blow on it to moisten it and then polished it once again.

The right breast had been left completely idle, but no sooner had I thought this than he stole that one as well.

Suddenly the thief gave me back my hand covered in white foam.

Then he offered me a handkerchief, and kept on saying "I'm sorry".

I ran away.

I go back to my room. People at the boarding house greet one another and then shut themselves in their rooms. I don't speak to anyone. I start writing and drawing.

The next day I'll go to a museum.

It's so difficult to wander around by myself. Even if I go to see a movie, there's always someone who sits next to me and within minutes has a hand in-side my shirt, as if that were absolutely normal. Yet I know I don't look like a whore. When I walked around with Baby it was easier. I miss Baby!

I miss the times when Baby and I strolled along the Arno. I'll never forget that cool evening, when the weather was nice and we sat listening to music. Baby and I are sitting at a bar by the river, where they're playing modern music, jazz. It's wonderful and we're very cheerful.

A tall, large man approaches our table, introduces himself as Mr Marcopulos and asks: "May I offer you a drink?"

He buys us two beers.

Baby is fascinated by him and asks: "Are you an artist?"

Yes, he says, he's an opera singer.

"I sing in Paris, London, New York. I sing everywhere. Now I'm in Italy."

"Really? My brother is a poet," she says, pointing at me.

I'd cut my hair very short and I was wearing trousers and a tie. Indeed, I was her twin brother. "Twins! How extraordinary! I immediately thought you must be two extraordinary individuals."

Baby says: "You seem like an extraordinary person yourself".

"So this is a young poet! I love artists. I can't bear the company of ordinary people," he says.

Marcopulos invites us to his home and we accept enthusiastically. He wants to show us photographs from his performances. He's preparing to be Othello.

"Who is the beautiful woman next to you, wearing that beautiful dress?"

"Desdemona," he says, "and this is Ophelia."

"Will you sing something for us, Mr Marcopoulos?" asks Baby.

The giant opens his mouth and produces a terrifying sound. I never would've thought he could make so much noise. He looks very satisfied and pours us cognac on ice. "No, Mr Marcopulos, don't give us more to drink, it's not good for us. I'm already feeling sick."

I stood up and staggered towards the bathroom. Mr Marcopulos helps me and lays me down on the bed, a large bed in a room lined with red velvet. It looks like a theatre. Othello is staring at me, his eyes fixed. He's enormous. As he leans over my body, I felt his large mass engulf me, and before I could free myself from his embrace he'd already unbuttoned my pants. I was about to scream when he jumped away from me, his face flushed and astonished, saying: "But you are a woman!"

In the small boarding house where I stay everyone greets each other morning and evening, but then they shut themselves in their rooms. If this were Italy, sooner or later you'd know something about everyone. In England, instead, silence reigns and non communication is the law. Self-control and respectability rule. Even in restaurants the silence is broken only by the clattering of forks and knives and the clinking of glasses. In Italy there would be mayhem. London is steeped in silence and in fog.

I always greet Professor Juilliar with a broad smile, because he always smiles back.

I so want to visit him, talk to him and show him the poems I wrote in French. One day I smile at him and ask: "May I come to see you?" Looking surprised, he answers: *"Mais oui, surement. Venez!"*

"I'd like to show you my poems in French. I'm afraid my grammar is poor. Could you correct them?"

"Mais bien sûr! Venez demain à cinq heures."

At five o'clock sharp I dash to the professor's door with my poems. I knock.

"Ah, je vous attendais, entrez, entrez, je vous en prie."

For the first time I see Professor Juilliar's room. It's far nicer than mine, a large room with a fireplace.

I feel slightly awkward, in fact very awkward. Standing there I no longer know what to say.

"Entrez, s'il vous plaît."

"C'est moi."
"Je le vois."

Professor Juilliar looks at me and says: *"Asseyez-vous, je vous en prie"*.

I sit on an armchair, so wide I could fit in it twice. The folder with my poems is under my arm.

Professor Juilliar sits down across from me and stares right at me. His long silences fascinate me.

"Vous aimez tourmenter les hommes!" he told me.

"Qui, moi?"

"Oui, vous."

Pause. Silence. He looks straight into my eyes smiling.

"Vous me troublez."

"Qui, moi?"

"Oui, vous."

Oh, Professor Juilliar speaks French so beautifully. I look into his eyes but can't say a word. He sits back and reads my poems.

I only want him to correct the poems I wrote in French, because surely there are mistakes.

On the mantelpiece I see photographs of a beautiful woman. "Is that your wife?" I ask.

"Yes," he replies.

I start talking about Baudelaire, saying how I read that he wanted to recite his poems to an audience and that he spent all his money on refreshments. When he sat down to read, the audience turned their backs on him, focusing on the food instead. So, he gave up reading and started eating with the others.

Wasn't that a sad story? Poor Baudelaire. Who knows how much he must have suffered? He too had a guardian who never sent him money.

I pick up a book from the professor's table.

"These lines are beautiful," I say.

He gets up from his chair, leans over the book and reads out loud: *"Loin du monde je vis tout seul comme un ermite enfermé dans mon coeur comme dans un tombeau".*

"It's by Valéry," he says, "he wrote this when he was fifteen."

"It's true Professor, we're all hermits, aren't we?" He isn't listening. He looks into my eyes, his face somehow pained and tormented. He moves away, towards the end of the room, still staring at me with those eyes and that solemn expression I find so fascinating.

"Are you not well Professor?"

The professor is very pale.

Pushing me gently towards the door, he says: "You must leave now, I don't have any more time today, and close the door behind you".

When I reach the door to the street, I realise I forgot my dictionary. Climbing the stairs four steps at a time, I arrive out of breath in front of his room. I ring the bell. Professor Juilliar opens the door. I apologise stuttering, saying that I forgot my dictionary on the table.

He takes me into his arms, holding me tight. He kisses me, he smothers me and covers me in kisses. Then he steps back and looks at me.

I stand there before him. I wait for what will happen next. For what is about to happen. Whatever that is. I just stand there waiting. The professor will decide. The professor is shaking. His hands tremble as he caresses me. His face is no longer his face. He has changed. Here is a man that holds me in his hands like an object whose colours and shapes I am seeing for the first time. I am that object in his arms.

I didn't know I had porcelain breasts that could shatter at a mere hand's touch. I didn't know I had cheeks of fire. I didn't know my ear against his chest could hear his heartbeat - a man's heartbeat is much louder that a woman's.

Professor Juilliar is a divinity that is transforming me into other things. I'm no longer myself, I'm transformed by his touch. My hair is seaweed and I grow branches and leaves.

He moves away. He looks at me, looks into my eyes and I see in his inner turmoil and in the changing expression of his face that something important is about to happen.

I'm a step away from life's mystery, but he sends me away with my dictionary and my blouse unbuttoned. Why?

Professor Juilliar is a gentleman.

In despair I call Baby. I still haven't received the money from the guardian. I'm happy to hear her voice.

"Hi Penny." She calls me Penny, like she used to do when we were little. "Stephen isn't here so we can finally talk and tell each other everything. How are you?"

"I'm desperate, I don't have a cent to my name, I keep waiting for money that doesn't come." Baby tells me crying: "We'll never get another lira from this guardian, he sold everything to go into business and lost it all."

"What do you mean, the whole country estate?"

"Yes."

"Even the Art Nouveau villa in Rome?"

"Yes."

"Even the villa in Cervia?"

"Everything. We can't even send him to jail, because we confirmed our trust in him when we came of age, and so it seems that we're also liable for bankruptcy."

"And how are you surviving?"

"Fortunately I found a job as a graphic designer with the publisher Sansoni. Federico Gentile, the son of the famous philosopher, runs the company and he's been very generous with me."

I step out of the phone booth where I've spent my very last coins and walk towards the boarding house where I've been staying for almost two months. For a while already I've been asked to pay up, and I keep telling them that the money is about to arrive.

One evening I return to the boarding house and find my suitcase, my drawings and the rest of my things on the pavement. I haven't paid the rent and they threw me out.

In vain I ask to be allowed back in my room. My request is denied. I truly don't know what to do. I sit on my suitcase and it starts to rain. It rains and I cry. *Il pleut dans mon coeur comme il pleut sur la ville...* Or was it perhaps, I wondered, *Il pleut sur la ville comme il pleut dans mon coeur?*

Who wrote that poem anyway?

It rains on me and on all my things. People walk by and no one says a word to me.

Suddenly I notice that the rain has stopped. There's a large black umbrella over me. It belongs to a young Japanese man who stands there smiling and sheltering me under his umbrella. He bends down and without a word picks up my suitcase and starts walking. I follow him in silence.

He takes me to his home, points to a small bed and makes me something to eat. He's very shy and he keeps bowing. I keep on crying as he gives me lots of little timid kisses, which make me cry even harder.

I'm not ready for calm and serenity. The only thing I'm probably ready for is the apocalypse. I need to call Baby.

III

Here I am. The employment agency has found me a beautiful little house with a garden - lovely. Yet I'm amazed to see a row of houses identical to it on either side of it, and across the street as well. I would never be able to recognise mine. I'm used to Florence and to Italy, where one's house is unique and forever recognisable. I knock, and a bejewelled woman comes to the door, wearing several sparkling necklaces.

I try to behave like a real maid, being extremely polite and deferential. I rush to say yes to everything she asks, and I nearly bow as a butler would to his master. I cannot let her find out about my right eye, the eye of truth, through which I look at her astonished, terrified at the mere thought of having anything at all to do with her.

After all, the more the butler maintains his distance, the more perfect he will be, and deference is the key element to all this.

She seemed slightly troubled by my exceedingly respectful manner, perhaps feeling that she was being denied a measure of friendship, which she preferred far more than deference. But you can't ask people to serve you and also expect them to give you their soul.

Breakfast at 7, wake up and breakfast with orange juice.

At 8, tea with toast and jam, followed by - and here things get more complicated - a poached egg. Using a special pot that makes the egg flat instead of round, you have to boil the egg until it's hard but not too hard, and then plop it on a piece of toast and heaven forbid if it breaks. The poached egg has to be placed on buttered toast and served with fork and knife.

I was extremely anxious, waking up during the night and mentally going through everything I had to do. At 7 o'clock I was ready with the orange juice.

I knock at the door and walk in maintaining my silent and deferential manner. I was hoping she'd smile, but I saw she wasn't satisfied. She told me to open the window and I obeyed, then locked myself in my room and started drawing while waiting for 8 o'clock.

I wonder: could I turn that picture that bothers me so much against the wall, or would that be rude? It was a painting of flowers, but the worst of it was the frame, studded with pieces of glittering glass, as if this woman's business was to sparkle. I was pretending to be a maid, and certainly playing a role, which any good actor should be able to do.

In order not to go insane I tried to trace my coordinates. I drew an "I" in the middle of a blank page and from it I traced lines, as in a spider's web, leading to the margins, where I wrote the names of objects, people and things for which I felt an affinity. I thought eventually this web of lines would represent my personality. Among the many lines that departed from my "I" and moved outward, was one that led to Lorenzo il Magnifico, since my name is Lorenza. Another one led to Botticelli, another to Kafka, and so on.

How could I live without Tolstoy, Dostoyevsky, and Kierkegaard, without Faulkner, Steinbeck, and Jesus?

I'd like to be with my friends, like Dante Alighieri when he says:

"Guido, I would that Lapo, thou, and I
Led by some strong enchantment, might ascend
A magic ship, whose charmed sails should fly
With winds at will where'er our thoughts might wend."

I'd like to be on that ship too, chatting with them, so I draw a line from my "I" to them as well. Camus is also very dear to me - I don't know whom I like better, whether Albert himself, who's so beautiful, or his character Mersault. However, Kafka is the one closest to me now, I even have his portrait above my bed. I am like him.

In The Trial, two characters visit K and announce that he's been condemned to death. There is no reason given for this death sentence, and if he wants one he must ask the Court.

In vain K goes from judge to judge asking for an explanation, but despite all the documents they read to him none exists. On the appointed day they come to take him away and they kill him.

Everybody finds this book mysterious, but I find it prophetic.

We too received a visit by two men who announced my uncle's death sentence. "What have I done wrong, why should I hide? Why should they kill me?" This is what my uncle said, and he kept desperately repeating this phrase until Aunt Nina pleaded with him to leave the house and escape into the woods.

He ran away, and when he came back, the house was on fire, and his wife and young daughters had been killed.

My uncle committed suicide.

Just as the two visitors wanted.

The Metamorphosis describes the desperation of a young man, who one morning can't go to work because he physically can't get out of bed.

He feels that his sense of guilt is transforming him into a non-human creature that horrifies his family. The father's shame and indignation towards the son are so great that he punishes him and leaves him to die inside a storage closet. The hate and scorn for him are such that, in the end, he is thrown out with the rubbish.

The young man actually can't bear to live a normal life, when normality and calm are for him just a form of indifference towards the horrors of the world, which become enveloped in sleep and in fog.

The Metamorphosis seems like a powerful act of accusation against the daily grind that makes us indifferent to past, present and future injustice.

It seems to me that Kafka often means to say exactly the opposite of what he writes.

Like him, I too can't accept being calm and serene, to eat, drink and sleep, because something inside me tells me I'm not allowed to have this serenity.

I've got to do something, but I don't know what, and yet I must, I must, I must. Still I don't know what. Seize a gun?

I couldn't finish my self-portrait because it was 8 o'clock and I had to serve my mistress her breakfast. I left the tray compliantly on her bedside table and tiptoed out of the room. Everything had been perfect but she wasn't satisfied, perhaps because she wanted me to stay and chat with her.

I returned to my room, sat down again at the table and traced a direct line from the "I" to a point I called "B," which stood for Baby, which is what I call my sister who stayed behind in Florence with her boyfriend.

"You must once and for all move away from each other, you can't live together forever. It's about time that the two of you separated". "No, I'll never separate from my sister..."

"Well why don't you marry her then!" That's what the idiot screamed.

While Lungarno delle Grazie is turning pink I'm here working as a maid for a woman who'd like me to talk to her. But she's not my mother. She's not even my adoptive mother, who rests in the cemetery of the Badiuzza in San Donato in Collina with her two daughters, my little cousins, and with Uncle Robert. The inscription on their gravestone reads 'Nina, Luce, Cicci Einstein massacred by the Germans'.

I'm ready to go food shopping and do anything else that needed to be done, but the bejewelled woman says that she wants to do the food shopping herself, and the cooking as well, so I hope that she will at least let me do the dishes.

Every day I would take refuge in my little room where I'd write, read or draw.

She became more and more curious about what I was doing behind that closed door.

I was still searching for the coordinates of my "I". So I traced a line from my "I" to the letter "N," which stood for Napoleon, one of the loves of my life. To think that he went down in history as a mere warmonger, when instead it was he who brought to Italy and Europe the fundamental values of human rights, proclaimed by the Enlightenment.

I love Napoleon, because when he arrived in Italy he freed the Jews from the ghettos and granted everyone freedom of religion.

The Pope got angry, however, and when Napoleon died he sent soldiers all over Italy with the task of capturing the liberated Jews to the cry of "Ave Maria" and locking them up once again in the ghettos. Then another pope wrote the Syllabus of Errors in which he defined the Jews as "barking dogs".

It took Mazzini, the Risorgimento, and Garibaldi to breach Porta Pia and tear down the walls of the Jewish ghetto.

This time the Pope was furious, and granted Father Ernest Jouin his placet to publish The Protocols of the Elders of Zion, a historical hoax claiming that the Jews were plotting to take over the world.

Hitler liked this libellous pamphlet so much that he had it reprinted.

Monsignor Jouin became a very important figure in the Vatican.

***

One Sunday I'm off from work and I go to an amusement park. When I get back I find the door to my room wide open, my papers scattered everywhere, and my mistress with two policemen rummaging through my only suitcase, which lay open on the bed.

They show me a silk petticoat. My mistress insists that it belongs to her and that I stole it, and since I'm a thief she wants me out.

The policemen suggest that I pack my suitcase and follow them, as my mistress no longer wants me in her house. I don't defend myself, don't even know enough English to do so. I'm speechless as I follow them out.

I'm a thief and I'm being banished.

The policemen escort me to an agency to find another place for me to stay.

What did I ever do? The bejewelled woman said I stole her lingerie. Huh?

Was I a thief?

Later I actually find out that the she is the thief. The ruby pendant that my uncle gave me for my birthday has disappeared. It belonged to Aunt Nina. A ruby drop lodged itself inside my heart.

***

I take the underground to go and find a job. My idea is to look for work as a waitress in a restaurant, or to place an ad for lessons in Italian or French, or respond to a classified ad that reads "Secretary wanted".

As I realise myself, I could never have made it as a secretary. All the other applicants might not be fluent in Italian or French, but they're well dressed, wear high heels, and don't walk around with a rucksack on their shoulders. I'm politely turned down. I do, however, receive a call from a man who is eager to learn Italian.

I'm very excited. It would be the first time that I earn something from my work.

I show up, sit down and, in an effort to look serious about what I'm about to do or say, I place books, papers and two pens on the table.

After almost a half an hour in which I try to get the man to repeat: *"Io amo tu ami egli ama."* Things aren't going very well, so I try with: *"Io uccido tu uccidi egli uccide"* and things only get worse. The man is attractive, wealthy, elegant, and he won't stop trying to kiss me. I finally ask him: "Are you interested in this lesson or not?" And he replies: "No, absolutely not".

I find myself walking down the street with my books and with my dignity as a teacher in crisis. I'm so tense that I end up taking the wrong underground train. I walk out, walk back in, and again think I'm on the right train but I'm not. The only satisfaction I have is that I haven't paid for the ticket. It's easy to enter the tube without one - you just have to crouch down and sneak in. If someone gives chase, you don't run but just hide in one of the many tunnels.

I finally sit down and relax, but I'm so tired that I miss my stop. I have to take the same train back in the opposite direction, and at the exit an inspector stops me and asks to see my ticket. Nervously, I stutter something to the effect of "I've lost it". He knows I'm lying just by looking at me, and demands my name and address. I give him the information - I'm staying with a woman who rents out rooms in her house.

One day I'm thrilled to receive mail, and it's the Underground in person writing me on a beautiful letterhead, asking me to show up on a given date for failing to pay the ticket several times. I'm summoned to appear in front of a judge.

In Italy you would never be called in front of a judge for such a trifle, but in England you are. What's more, the judge sits on a throne-like seat wearing a black tunic, and a wig on his head that reminds me a lot of Robespierre.

"You failed to pay your underground ticket several times, do you realise this is a repeat offence?" says the judge.

Before he can continue his sermon I shout "No! I'll never do it again!" and burst out crying, and keep on repeating the phrase over and over just as the kind policeman has advised me to do.

Robespierre is taken by surprise and is moved. To think that I would've gone in and said that after all, not paying a ticket was not such a serious offence!

To my surprise I can't stop crying and go on sobbing uncontrollably. People gather around me, but their words and caresses are to no avail, I relentlessly continue to sob.

Once the tears are uncorked, repressed pain runs rampant.

The judge leans over, strokes my head and says: "Well, now, it's unnecessary to get so worked up over an unpaid ticket," and gives me a pat on the cheek. I find myself in the arms of the policeman who had advised me to cry.

***

I finally found work with a caring and educated family who live in a beautiful house. The husband is a youthful looking university professor with grey hair, and the wife is an attractive blonde woman who takes care of their daughters. They are all good-looking and kind. There are flowers on the wife's dress, flowers on the dining table, flowers in the garden.

It's a triumph of colours, sweetness and lullabies that I once knew well myself.

They go outside with baskets to pick raspberries in the garden.

We too went to pick blackberries in our floral dresses, singing: "O Tannenbaum, o Tannenbaum, wie grun sind deine Blatter..." Baby and I and Cicci would sing together.

With our little baskets we, too, went looking for berries.

I go to call Luce, to tell her to come with us.

Luce is in front of the mirror combing her hair. I call her but she just keeps on combing her hair. So I go over to Aunt Nina and ask her to come with us, but my aunt is combing her hair. She doesn't look at me and doesn't answer, she keeps combing her hair in silence.

Baby and I go out alone but it's so difficult - where are the blackberries, where are the bushes? This is a desert, we are walking in the sand, we've lost our way. Where is our home? I woke up in London.

The couple are very nice and ask me to dine with them. My eyes well up with tears, the table is set, the children offer the raspberries they picked, everyone is happy and they ask me again to dine with them. Here I am, the maid, and I can't bear that much happiness when there is a void in my soul. I ran away and never went back.

With my suitcase I run away in search of some unhappiness. I stop in front of a restaurant. I'm cold. I go in and order eggs and bacon and later offer to work as a waitress. I'm hired to wash dishes by a waiter by the name of Hamed.

I work two days a week, during which I stuff myself with food, thinking I can go without eating the other five days.

I finally found my unhappiness. I couldn't have chosen a gloomier place.

I'm reduced to snatching a pound I find on the floor, but Hamed sees it too and says it's his because he saw it first. Like good friends we split it in half, he gives me five shillings and keeps the pound.

When I go back to my room, I realise that it had been my last pound, which had fallen out of my pockets.

***

I'm cold, I'm hungry and I'm enveloped in the fog, which is more like smog, saturated with the smoke of all the chimneys of London's buildings and of the underground.

In the darkness of the street I see a small flickering light. I move towards it. It's a restaurant. How I envy the people sitting in that warmth, eating. I wish I could be inside too; instead my hands ache from the cold and I shiver all over. I press my face against the glass, through which I can delight in the happiness of others. I feed on their wine and roast meat, and the aroma is so strong it feels as if I too am eating the roast.

Dazzled by this miracle I open my eyes and find myself in my room. The room is filled with the same aroma of the dream. I think it can't be true, but it is.

I step out and realise that the scent is rising from the rooms on the ground floor. I climb down the stairs and find myself in front of a door. It's ajar and I push it open, and I'm presented with an amazing sight: an enormous steaming bowl set on a square table, surrounded by smiling children and adults who beckon me to come in.

They greet me, sit me down and invite me to eat with them, laughing and joking and playfully urging me on. They hug me and it makes me cry.

I dry my tears on the napkin, pretending to wipe my mouth. I eat cheerfully and smile, finally.

I discover that this amazing food I've never tasted before, this divine ambrosia, is called curry, and that these lovely people are from India.

***

I find another job at the Soup Kitchen, a restaurant that serves mostly soups - tomato soup, pea soup, vegetable soup - but also omelettes with onion, mushroom or cheese, as well as various desserts.

The soups are served in bowls with bread and butter on the side. Popular with the theatre crowd, the restaurant is in the heart of London at Charing Cross. I'm finally eating every day. I have to call Baby to tell her, tell her not to worry anymore because I'm eating every day.

I ring Baby and her boyfriend is still insisting on this absurdity - that twins must learn to live apart.

Baby and I hold hands and roll down in the green grass. So nice!

"Hey, there's no stepping on the wheat," says Peppone, "I'm going to tell the Master!"

"No! Don't tell Uncle Robert, please!"

We scamper off as he chases us.

Baby and I tell lies. We say we didn't break the beautiful Murano vase and, hoping the Virgin Mary will come to our rescue, we pray to her intensely. The Virgin Mary didn't fix the vase, so doubts on the existence of God began to show in my right eye as well, but Baby said: "No, we simply didn't pray hard enough". Uncle Robert made us write forty times: "No ball playing in the living room".

Baby and I pee, perched on a tree branch. What a thrill! We are two birds and we can't speak, so we can't answer when the grown-ups call for us, and so we got punished.

We were sent to bed without pudding and also without chicken and without pasta. But we never went to sleep without eating, because Aunt Nina would always secretly bring up something for us. What I regretted most of all, however, was not getting a goodnight kiss. I would've happily traded a portion of pudding for a kiss.

I would've given up my coloured stones, my largest multi-coloured marble, and then a little piece of my left pinkie, a little piece of my big toe, and an ear, but would've kept my eyes to see my uncle's face as he bent down over me and said: "Good girl!"

How can you send a child to bed without kissing her goodnight, knowing that it means the world to her?

My heart would pound when our bedroom door opened and in the shaft of light I'd see the silhou-

Lorenza Mazzetti, Daniele Paris, John Fletcher and a friend on a London street

earrings, or rings. She would show up as she was, with her blond hair and blue eyes, smiling and filled with a subtle sense of humour. Everyone was infatuated with her, including us. Just as the Virgin Mary intercedes with God for mankind, so Aunt Nina interceded with Uncle Robert for us, convincing him to forgive our mischief.

If our aunt wriggled her little finger while we sat at the table, she was warning us children that he was in a bad mood.

Uncle Robert was in a bad mood because an ox had died and there was no money to buy another one, and without an ox you couldn't plough the land.

Please forgive me if I was a little harsh with you. Don't forget me, and don't forget Aunt Nina, Cicci, Luce, and the things we taught you. Your Uncle Robert."

P.S. Don't wear mourning.

IV

"Can I buy you a drink?" I'm in London. A young man looks at me kindly, offers me a drink and asks me to dance. The club is very crowded, and there's a round lamp in the middle of the hall reflecting the coloured lights.

The noise and chaos are phenomenal. The orchestra starts playing and everyone moves to the middle of the floor to dance the boogie-woogie, the new American dance that is all the rage among young people in this slumbering London. We dance until late. The shy and kind young man asks to see me again. He works all day as a shop assistant and is free on Saturday nights. I happily accept to see him again with his friends. He leaves looking like a Little Lord Fauntleroy, so elegant in his grey coat with a black velvet collar.

All the young people dress this way. With mild disdain, the newspapers and the upper class call them Edwardians or Teddy Boys, but they are the heartbeat of London.

***

I decide that I can't spend my life washing dishes. I gather the drawings I've been obsessively making at night and bring them to the Slade School of Fine Art at University College London, to attend their classes. I arrive and introduce myself. A very poised and well-mannered young lady greets me, and with a smile informs me of the various reasons why I can't enrol in the college. To begin with, the academic year starts on the following day and I haven't completed the necessary requirements for admission. Secondly, I haven't taken the preliminary exam or filled out an application. Thirdly, my English is inadequate for admission, so with another smile she asks me to leave.

I'm thinking there's no way I'm leaving, I'll never leave here. I'll stay put, and they'll have to call the police. The young lady insists, and smiling once again asks me to leave.

I start shouting that I have a right to see and speak to the director before I leave. I raise my voice even more and she also raises hers, but I'm louder still, and to my great surprise, she raises hers even louder.

Finally a door opens and an extremely thin fellow in shirtsleeves, wearing braces and black over-sleeves like the ones used by 19th-century scribes, inquires as to the reason for the mayhem. In her eloquent and impeccable English the smiling young lady explains that this young woman - pointing at me - wishes to enrol in the university but hasn't completed the required procedures.

I intervene shouting that I must talk to the director. I only want to speak to him and I won't leave until I do so.

The thin fellow with blondish hair and a narrow face motions for me to follow him. Clearly he's taking me to the director, I think, and indeed he ushers me into a room. He asks what it is that I want to tell the director.

Not knowing what to say, in order to obtain a meeting I blurt out: "I'm a genius". Amused by my answer, he says: "Let me have a look at your drawings".

I open my folder and show them to him. He seems interested and tells me: "Very well, starting tomorrow you'll be our student".

Lorenza Mazzetti

"Yes, thank you, but I'd like to speak to the director."

He smiles at me with his sharp and witty face and says: "I am the director".

I never thought I'd find a director who didn't behave like a director, who followed his intuition rather than the rules, who'd accept students on merit and not on how well they fill out an application.

How I love him. I'm completely in love with him.

The next morning at 9:30 sharp, he's standing at the top of the staircase as promised. As I arrive I'm so nervous that I fall on the stairs with all my odds and ends. He descends, bends down to pick up pencils, paintbrushes, colours, and papers, and without saying a word points the way for me.

I promise myself that I'll show Sir William Coldstream who I am.

Attending this art school is an experience like no other - one meets the oddest individuals among both professors and students. There's a young professor by the name of Lucian Freud and people tell me he's the grandson of Sigmund Freud. He seems unapproachable, but his look is not so much intimidating as terrified. It reminds me of the terrified look on the face of Franz Kafka, whose picture hangs on the wall of my tiny room. The room is so small it can fit only a bed besides my beloved Franz.

Professor Wittkower seems affable and compassionate. His art history classes are crowded with students and full of slide projections. I'm quite fond of them.

The students too are all a bit strange. The way they dress is inventive and they're always wearing something unique.

The girls are stunning, often wearing wide skirts with small floral patterns and ballet flats. Among the students there's a tall, thin, lanky young man who seems to have his head in the clouds. He's extremely kind and I wonder how he survives in the real world without snapping in two like a twig. His naivety is not accidental but chosen - it's his way of making a masterpiece out of himself. His name is Michael Andrews.

***

I wander down the many hallways of the university. I come across a series of small doors, each with a sign for a different club.

Tennis Club, Dance Club, there's even a Chess Club.

Just as I'm thinking I should join a club I reach a door with the sign "Film Club". Trembling with excitement, I slowly open the door and there I see the treasure. It sparkles, and my immediate desire is to steal it, but I'm also terrified that someone will see me. I shut the door and run.

I intend to return with my friends and take what I need. It's a matter of stealing the treasure and walking away.

I go in search of Michael. I find him working on his painting, as is everyone else and as I should be doing myself.

I'm struck and fascinated by his painting. It depicts men and women in bathing suits lying on a sandy beach. Both the sky and the sea are the colour of lead, although the sea is calm. In the left foreground, a large man stands with his back nearly turned to the viewer, gazing motionless at the beach. He is impeccably dressed in a grey suit and shiny shoes, and is enormous compared to the other figures. The effect is one of alienation.

The idea of the outsider strikes me. It reminds me of Camus' stranger. I love the painting and say so to Michael, then add: "I've found a treasure, it's a secret. Come, follow me".

I lead him down that attic hallway to the treasure's small door and tell him: "Look!" and I open the door. He looks, but doesn't quite understand. What is it? So I ask him how he would feel about acting in a short film. He smiles.

Here in this room is all that's needed to shoot a film: camera, tripods, film, lights, everything. All we have to do is take it and carry it out.

I also ask Hamad Hadary, the young Egyptian photographer, if he wants to participate in the shoot. He's thrilled to be part of the group and to be making a film.

Michael will carry the tripod, Hamad the camera and I will take the film. We'll meet at the end of Gower Street and from there bring everything to my room. We'll leave separately, one at a time, each carrying a bag.

***

Everything is under the bed in my tiny room: camera, tripod, film, lamps and lights.

I am really anxious, Franz Kafka is looking at me and I so understand his look of terror. He's my friend, because when I no longer know who I am I come back to this little room and always find him here.

He and I have one thing in common. Terror. We both have terror in our eyes. He's seen it through the eyes of his prophet and I've seen it in real life. We're the same.

***

I describe to Michael the story of the film I want to make, based on Franz Kafka's short story The Metamorphosis.

Michael isn't familiar with Kafka and wants to know more.
"Give me the script so I can read it and memorise it."

"No, you don't have to memorise anything." "What? There's no script?" "No, you just need to try to get out of bed, but you can't because all your little legs start moving at once." "What? Little legs?"
"Listen, he's imagining that he's got many little legs."

"And how does it end?"

"It's not important for me to tell you how it ends."

"But I want to know!"

"You see, his parents lock him up in a small room, actually in a closet, because they're ashamed of him. They live off the rent from the rooms they lease and it's important that Gregor, the protagonist, remain hidden from the paying guests."

"Yes, but how does it end?"

"I'm not telling you."

"I want to know."

"Well, he dies and gets thrown out with the rubbish."

Michael's jaw drops open.

"But you must understand," I say, "the author's message is the exact opposite of what he's writing. What matters is the impact this has on the audience. Gregor is the outcast, but with his death he becomes the accuser. Like Jesus, after all. There are people with damaged souls, Michael, who sometimes struggle to find the energy to live. Like me, for example."

"What are you saying?"

He smiles and hugs me. "Don't be silly!"

"So, Michael, are you going to act for me or not?"

"Ok, ok!" He holds me tight…

***

Michael and I go out together to Portobello Road, the antiques market near my place full of fascinating things like old photographs, plates, lamps, pillows, blankets, furniture, and paintings from the late 1800s and early 1900s.

I'd like to buy everything.

I stop to talk with the owner of a stall and as we chat I ask him where he puts his stuff at night when the market shuts down. He tells me he stores it not far from there.

He has a photo I want to buy, but the glass is too expensive. Does he have one that costs less? Yes, perhaps in storage. He opens a door and my heart starts pounding: here's the treasure!

Box springs leaning against the walls, stacks of old paintings, a broken down couch. A real treasure! This is where I'll shoot my film.

"We are shooting a film," I tell him. "Could we film a scene in your storage space? It's perfect for our story."

"But I can't move the furniture out," says the owner.

"I like it exactly as it is, with all the furniture piled up."

"What film, what's it about?" "It's based on a short story by Franz Kafka." "Don't know him."

"A great writer," I say.

"But what's it about?"

"It's about a young man who can't get up, because he can't climb out of his bed."

"That's not new! All the kids complain when they get up in the morning. But what does my storage space have to do with your film?"

"Well, his parents punish him by locking him in a storage room."

"And how does it end?"

"Very happily. He gets up, goes to school, gets excellent grades and then gets married!"

"Ah, a kids' writer. Right then, it's a deal." "But we can't pay you."

"It doesn't matter, I've got kids myself." "Thanks a million. We'll see you tomorrow then." As we are walking away, he shouts: "What's the name of the short story?".

"The Metamorphosis," I answer.

"I'll buy it tomorrow," he says and waves good-bye.

We smile and wave back.

A wonderful smell of sausages is coming from the end of the street. We order two each. How great it is to eat when you're hungry!

***

The next day we all meet in Professor Wittkower's class. He's a big man who enthrals his students with lectures filled with slide projections. There's total silence and the audience is rapt.

I search for my actors among the students. There are many interesting faces. After focusing on Gregor Samsa and getting Michael to agree to play the part, I need to find the other characters. I see a blond student with a beard and a Romantic demeanour evoking Foscolo and Lord Byron, and I ask him to play the guest. He readily accepts, as all he'll need to do is sit in an armchair. Another student, a beautiful friend of mine, also agrees to participate. She asks me what it will entail and I say: "Nothing, you'll only need to play the violin". "But I don't know how to play", she answers. "It doesn't matter, just pretend."

Now I'm only missing the manager of the company Gregor Samsa works for.

I walk into a wholesale fabric shop and ask for the manager. He's not in. It's an extraordinary shop, filled with aisles and bolts of fabric, all very dusty. It would be an ideal set for Gregor Samsa.

A clerk informs me that Mr Lowensberg, the manager, will be back shortly. I position myself next to the entrance. As I wait, I nervously gear up to ask him to act for me and to lend me his office.

At last I see a rather large man with a bowler hat approaching. I want to be extremely polite. I bow and ask: "Mister Lowensberg, I presume?". He looks astonished. I repeat: "Mister Lowensberg, I suppose". He smiles and says "Mister Lowensberg". In a fluster I tell him why I came. He agrees right away, adds that it won't be a problem and that he'll even act for me but that I must explain everything in detail. I'm so happy I could hug him, but he's so large and imposing that I restrain myself.

Mazzetti, Anderson, Chapaltine and Harris

He walks me around the whole studio, and then arranges to meet me in half an hour at a cafe across the street to talk more.

I take a seat in the large café-restaurant, where waitresses wearing black uniforms with white aprons and lace serve everyone coffee with milk. I'm surprised to see that here in London people don't drink wine but coffee and milk with their steaks!

Mr Lowensberg joins me and orders a steak with coffee and milk. It's my turn, but I have no money and don't know what to ask for, so I don't eat. Mr. Lowensberg ends up ordering a steak and coffee with milk for me as well.

After several preambles, I explain to him that I need his face, his hat and coat, his umbrella and his office to shoot a scene from a short story by Kafka. "Kafka," he repeats, "and who is this Kafka?"

I would rather not tell him anything but he insists, and I'm so flustered I can't eat or cut my steak. I'll have to tell him that Gregor Samsa's character is a travelling salesman who dearly loves his employer, but loves him so much he can't get out of bed. Yet I'm quick to point out that it's not because he doesn't want to go to work, he's just unable to get there. When they knock at his door, he answers: "I'm coming, I'm coming, I'm coming". His father, mother and sister keep calling him and he tells them: "I'm coming, I'm coming, I'm coming," but falls from the bed on his back and is unable to flip himself over with his little legs.

At this point Mr. Lowensberg opens his eyes wide, but I reassure him that the salesman eventually manages to flip himself over.

He still asks: "What's with the little legs?"

Here I stutter something or other about Kafka being the greatest author of the century, even greater than Shakespeare and Dante Alighieri, simply a genius, until Mr Lowensberg, embarrassed about never having read Kafka, says: "Yes, yes, I understand". Then, looking slightly annoyed: "You haven't touched your steak!"

I mumble that I'm too nervous to eat, so with an authoritative gesture he summons the waitress and asks her to wrap up the steak for me. He puts the package in my bag.

"Thank you so much," I say.

***

I now have the main protagonists for Kafka's The Metamorphosis. Michael will be Gregor Samsa and Mr Lowensberg will be his boss.

The beautiful Mary, a student at the Slade, will be Gregor's sister. Peter, so elegant and self-controlled, will be one of the paying guests. I'm still missing Gregor's father and mother.

I return to the neighbourhood of Portobello Road, where I've found the storage space where Gregor is confined.

Now I need the living room.

I ring at various doors and finally meet a lovely lady who's happy to help me out. She'll lend me her own sitting room for the final scene and offers to play the piano herself. I've found the living room, the piano, and Gregor's mother as well. I'm missing the father.

I need someone imposing, with a beard and a stern appearance. I suddenly think of Professor Claude Rogers.

When I go to his class I ask him if he'd be willing to act for three minutes for me. To my surprise he agrees. The British people are truly extraordinary!

**

It was a bit difficult to convince Michael that he didn't have to act but only struggle to get out of bed and crawl across the floor in his nightshirt without reciting Shakespeare.

He had agreed because I told him that Kafka was a very influential figure, although he had never even heard of him.

I knew about Kafka because Uncle Robert and Aunt Nina would discuss his writings at the table with Professor Paoli, who taught German at the University of Florence and who brought them this book when it was first published.

The book had shaken our whole family. Hiding behind the door, I would listen to the strange story of Gregor Samsa and it made a lasting impression on me.

Then when I saw a picture of the young Kafka I was shocked by his eyes and by his thin, delicate, sensitive, and fragile face, and I fell in love with him. In order to feel alive it is important to love. So what am I doing here in this strange black city enveloped in the fog and in the smell of the smog that permeates everybody's clothes?

To feel alive means having a connection to another living being, especially when I don't identify with anyone around me. I pretend to joke and laugh while the others are laughing for real. Why can't I? The others can and I can't. It's not even that I can't. I'm not allowed to.

I ask myself: Who am I? What am I doing here? This isn't my country, it isn't my home. I have no one in the world - they're all dead.

My sister has married and is expecting a baby. When I'm with her I'm in the way, but how can a twin live far away from her own twin?

***

During the first day, we shot the scenes with Mr Lowensberg until Mr Lowensberg wanted to stop and go to a restaurant because he was hungry.

We followed him and watched him eat. None of us had any money. In the end he broke down and invited us to join him, so the first day of shooting ended well. On the second day we didn't have Mr Lowensberg, hence we had no lunch, but to make up for this we had Professor Claude Rogers, who taught painting at the Slade School. At the right moment he played his part: he got up, took the apples from the table and threw them at Gregor Samsa. I'll be eternally grateful to him for this, Gregor a little less so...

***

After adding a few more scenes I brought all the film to be developed at the lab on the same street as the University College, telling them that it was university film that needed to be developed.

Once I picked up the film I brought it to my tiny room to edit it. I needed to put the scenes in sequence, joining the film as follows: I scratched the ends of the film which needed to be joined together with a razor blade, added a drop of a mysterious liquid on one end, stuck the other end on top of the first, lowered a lever that pressed the two together and waited at least five minutes. And lo and behold the miracle happened. Using my bed as a table I placed the machine on top of it, edited the film and then happily fell asleep.

The partisans are coming, through the window I see people moving in the bushes and the bayonets glinting in the sun. And I say: "They're coming to save us, they're on their way". But they never seem to arrive. "Here they come, they're about to come, they're just steps away, here they are!" The door opens, but it's not the partisans, it's the SS. I wake up.

I have to call Baby. I gather all the coins I can find and walk to a phone booth. Baby tells me that her job is going well and that she and Stephen have turned our house into a modern art gallery.

"We're having a Giacomo Balla exhibit, then we'll be showing Rauschenberg, Piero Dorazio and Perilli, who are also giving us a hand in organising the shows. They're all living here with us and many other painters are passing through. No one can be denied a plate of spaghetti!"

"Did you see Giacomo Balla?" I ask her.

"Yes, I went to Rome to see him. He hugged me tight and his daughters Elica and Luce were really happy to see me again, and selected the paintings for the show. But they were saddened by the deaths of Uncle Robert, Aunt Nina and our little cousins."

I'm happy for the news Baby is giving me and I tell her about the short Kafka film.

I ask her to get in touch with Daniele Paris, a musician friend of ours, to let him know that I'm waiting for the recorded tape with the music we spoke about on the phone, that is the modern piece and the poignant violin solo piece. "Tell him it must be really poignant, because it's for the ending of the film. And also please remind Jacopo Treves of the monologue I asked of him, the one where K apologises to his boss and promises to get up and go to work as soon as he can. Tell him to send it as soon as possible."

Baby tells me not to worry as she has already sent me everything a couple of days before!

The next day I receive the tape with Daniele Paris's music from Florence. It's quite beautiful. Jacopo's English text for the monologue is also excellent.

I call Michael and ask him to read it out loud because I need to record it.

I rush to the film lab with all the tapes and explain to the technician where to add the music and where to add the monologue.

The violin music has to begin as soon as the living room door opens. Gregor then enters the living room crawling across the carpet, attracted by the melody. He moves forward unseen by the guests who are listening to the concert. The melody becomes more heart wrenching, reminding Gregor of the times when he was like everyone else.

But Gregor crawls too far inside the room. How dare he?

His father sees him and stands up, then everyone else sees him and they leap to their feet, filled with horror. At this point the violin has to stop.

"It is a rather complicated job," says the technician.

"Yes, but it's very urgent," I tell him, "and please remember to add the monologue at the beginning when the protagonist follows his boss."

"Excuse me, but how do you expect me to synchronize the lips? It has to be dubbed."

"No, no. They're just thoughts in voice-over." "All right, no synchronization! In any case, it's going to cost quite a bit."

"No worries, no worries, it's for the university." "Oh, very well. Would you mind signing here?" He hands me some papers and I sign everywhere he asks me to, on behalf of University College London. Then I leave very happy to have finished the film.

I deserve a meal. I rush out to find a fish and chips vendor. Who invented this wonderful meal? I leave with my newspaper cone full of fried fish and potatoes.

How great it is to eat when you're hungry.

***

Today is Shrove Tuesday and there are celebrations at the university.

I arrive to find all the lights on, everyone in fancy dress and a band playing. To the side there are refreshments and drinks.

All the costumes are very elaborate and truly extraordinary, so I can't recognise anybody and I'm a little disoriented. I look for my friends but I can't see them. I have to uncover them.

All of a sudden I see a Pierrot who is identical to the young Jean-Louis Barrault in Les Enfants du Paradis. It's Michael!

I run towards him and he stoops to hug me. I tell him that with that mask and his face all white he looks a lot like Jean-Louis Barrault in Les Enfants du Paradis, but he knows neither Jean-Louis Barrault, nor Marcel Carné.

Two carnival-goers make their entrance through the main door: a man with the head of a white cat who is talking animatedly to a tall, large gypsy lady with two very large round breasts and a turban on her head.

"Who are those two?" I ask Michael.

"Lori, can't you see it's Principal Coldstream and Professor Wittkower?"

My jaw drops open. In this university intelligence and sense of humour triumph. The orchestra starts playing. We dive onto the dance floor and alternate dancing with beer drinking breaks.

After a while my head is spinning. Am I really having trouble standing up?

"To bed, to bed! Everyone off to bed!"

"No, no!" we scream, "Not to bed!"

"Oh yes, a fun game can't last forever. Now everyone go to bed and be quiet!" This is how our uncle would ship us off to bed, suddenly becoming serious and unbending in his decision.

I never wanted to go to bed, but all that curbing of my exuberance gave me such a sense of safety. Now no one tells me to go to bed when I drink too much and feel sick. My head is spinning and I can barely stand up.

Pierrot leans towards me and says: "Enough now, it's time to go to bed!"

***

After a few days, William Coldstream calls for me and asks me: "Did you sign these documents on behalf of the College?" Looking straight into my eyes he adds: "In England you go to prison if you falsify a signature".

"Yes, I did."

The principal then asks me: "Are you going to pay for this?"

"No, I don't have a penny."

"I'm terribly sorry, but you shall have to go to prison".

"All right," I say leaving.

He called me back, wanting to know why on earth I needed to spend so much money on printing and developing. I told him I had made a short film based on Franz Kafka's The Metamorphosis.

"Who gave you the camera? And the film stock?" I answered that I got them from the university's Film Society.
"Ah... You'll have to pay for those as well."

"May I go now?"

Lorenza Mazzetti, Daniele Paris, John Fletcher, Lindsay Anderson having a tea break while making Together. *Courtesy of Stirling University Anderson Collection.*

"No," says the principal, "I'd like to have a look at your film before I send you to prison. The students will decide whether you should be sent or not, either by cheering or booing".

The wretched day finally arrived. The auditorium was crammed with students. During the screening I was so anxious I had a stomach ache and kept vomiting. It seemed like a horrible film, what had I done? I deserved to go to prison. It was then that the lights came on and I heard the applause. I couldn't believe my ears.

I looked from the highest semicircle of seats and saw William Coldstream with a handsome gentleman climbing the steps towards me.

"Lorenza, I'd like to introduce you to Denis Forman, the director of the British Film Institute. He'd like to have a word with you."

The tall and dashing gentleman bent down to shake my hand saying: "Would you like to make a film without having to go to prison?"

"Yes, of course."

"Then come to the British Film Institute tomorrow for tea, so we can have a chat, and bring me an idea for the next film, no more than a page."

***

The following day, at the University, I meet the young Lucian Freud. He would usually look at everybody with an elusive and diffident expression, instead there he is smiling at me, shaking my hand and even telling me he hopes to act in my next film based on Kafka.

On closer view, Lucian Freud truly has the terrified look of someone who sees in his fellow man or in his surroundings something horrific and appalling.

Even the famous critic John Berger comes over to congratulate me, being very kind and affectionate. He has beautiful features, blond hair and romantic blue eyes which he conceals behind glasses.

At five o'clock I rush to my appointment with Denis Forman at the British Film Institute on Shaftesbury Avenue.

I'm a little late and arrive out of breath. I ask for the director and someone points to his office door. I walk in and find a small table set for tea with two cups, a steaming teapot and biscuits.

My guardian angel invites me to sit down on one of the small chairs and promptly asks me if I brought him the page with my idea for a new film.

I take out the page, but I'm in such a state that I bump into the small table. The hot tea spills on his knee. I freeze, thinking: what have I done?

I've burned the leg of my guardian angel, the man who would've opened the doors to my future, the man who smiles kindly at me and even offers me biscuits! I stand there paralysed witnessing the scene, screaming:

"I'm sorry, I'm sorry, I'm sorry!"

Instead of getting angry, the angel smiles and says:

"Don't worry, my leg is wood," and as he raps against it I hear the sound of it. Still smiling, he adds: "I left my leg in Cassino, Italy".

My angel had lost his leg in Cassino fighting for us Italians. And there he was sitting across from me, offering me sweets, reading what I wrote and saying: "Very well, it's a great idea, you can start shooting your next film tomorrow".

V

Scouting for locations for my next film, I cross the
Thames and visit the East End for the first time. I
arrive at a vast flat area, an expanse of some sort.
It's not quite a square because it's full of potholes.
The fog is so thick that I can't see where it ends.
There is a mysterious screeching of birds, which
suddenly gets louder and then just as suddenly
disappears. What a strange place.

I know this is London, but it feels as if I landed in
some fairy tale with ogres and witches. As I walk
on, the noise gets louder. It could be a large flock
of small birds coming together and then flying
apart. These aren't birds, however, they're
screaming children! They're running everywhere,

swarming together and then suddenly disappearing left and right, only to reappear again shrieking.

"Where am I?"

I walk further, I trip and fall in a hole in the pavement, get up and run after a boy who shrieks and squeals as he disappears into the fog. I see them in the distance, gathered together once again. I walk towards them, but at a signal they scatter in all directions.

I'm fascinated. Perhaps they're speaking English with a typical childish lilt. Their voices create a kind of musical refrain, so different from the sound made by Italian kids.

Here the children have found their own kingdom. Hitler's bombs left them a gift, a large space all for themselves in the heart of the city.

As I'm thinking that this could be a good film location, I realise it's getting dark. Groping around, I reach a row of houses where I hope someone will tell me about this place and show me a way out. I'm obviously lost, I don't know which direction I came from, and the fog is so thick that I can't see the end of this very long and straight road. Strange iron bridges connect the houses on the right with those on the left.

There are no doorbells, so I knock on a door then knock again two, three times, but nobody answers.

I move to the next door and knock again. The windows are shuttered. I have ended up on a completely empty imaginary road immersed in the fog! I notice that every house is numbered. Darkness is about to fall and I'm getting scared.

I no longer hear the children. Lost on a deserted street, I start running, hoping to meet another human being.

I hear footsteps. A little man holding a long stick runs past me, completely ignoring me. He's holding the stick up high and I see him stop at a corner of the street to light a gas lamp!

A feeble light illuminates the area and the little man starts running again. He runs to light up another gas lamp. Where am I? So it's true, this is a fairy tale... Suddenly I hear music, but where is it coming from? It's coming from the end of the street.

Enticed by the sound, I run towards it, trip and fall again, stand up and notice a low wall separating two houses. I walk to the wall, look beyond it and see the river! Leaning over it, I see thousands of cranes in ghostly stillness.

This has to be the Port of London, I think. I start running to catch up with the little man who keeps lighting the gas lamps and seems to lead me towards the music. I've reached the music!

It's a pub. I peep inside the glass door, but don't dare to go in. There is a giant black man dancing to a jazz groove from a juke-box, while other men stand around drinking - they look like dock workers, some are Indian, and one wears a turban.

Holding a glass, a big burly man walks to the centre of the room and starts to sing dreadfully out of tune. He looks completely drunk and, with his voice choking, attempts to generate what's supposed to be a melody. I still don't have the courage to go in, but two small older women nudge me inside as they enter. The two women greet the others and settle down in front of a glass of beer. Other men come in. From the many slaps on the back being exchanged, I deduce that they all know each other. Fortunately everyone's level of intoxication is such that I go unnoticed.

An old man turns to me and blows his beer breath in my face as he talks enthusiastically about something I obviously don't understand, but I smile, feigning great interest.

I think this is certainly the place where I'll shoot my film. Tomorrow morning I'll come back to see it in the daytime.

I can't remember how I got home, but the following morning I was back there. The little birds were still there, running and screaming.

I'm thrilled to find the street looking completely changed from the previous evening.

The doors are wide open and men are leaning out of the windows, shouting as they heave up and lower sacks and boxes. Other men are pushing trolleys filled with merchandise across the iron bridges, from one building to the next.

The din of shouting men, screaming children, roaring trolleys and squeaking pulleys is interspersed by the dull sirens of the ships.

I lean out over the low wall and see barges crowding the river, and the cranes lifting containers from the barges and moving them into the numbered houses that had frightened me the night before.

It's an amazing concert of voices and sounds. My two actors, playing deaf-mute characters, won't hear it, and the noisy world will be soundless through their eyes.

Still from Lorenza Mazetti's film Together *(1956)*

What do I mean to say with all this?

The following day I called the friends who shot K with me - the cameraman Hamad Hadary and Michael Andrews.

I asked Michael if he could act in my new film. Delighted, he wanted to know what his lines were, and I answered: "Look, you won't have to say anything". "What? I won't have to say anything?" "Yes, because your character is deaf-mute."

I only needed a second actor to play the other deaf-mute. My idea was to place these two characters within a world completely different from theirs, so that the film could switch back and forth between silence and sound, without needing any dialogue.

The only thread running through the film would be the children swarming the areas of London bombed by Hitler. Moving like gnats, they ran and screamed with their little voices, creating an ideal contrast to the silent world of the two protagonists, who walked past those ruins every day.

I didn't quite understand what I wanted to say with this story, I only knew that I was very taken by the idea of two people immersed in a world that they were not aware of and that ignored them.

After all, I really felt like an outsider, and being a twin I felt like a double, but wasn't quite sure of what I wanted to say.

I found the sight of Michael next to Eduardo Paolozzi very moving, because one was thin and the other large and they reminded me of the Pasztor brothers, who steal marbles from the children of the camp in Ferenc Molnár's The Paul Street Boys.

***

I'd met Eduardo Paolozzi at the Hanover Gallery, where I was astounded to see four paintings that portrayed the pope without eyes and with only a mouth, on a lilac background. They were by an artist called Francis Bacon. Being Italian, the figure of the pope couldn't leave me cold, especially when portrayed in such an extraordinary fashion. I realised that this painter, Francis Bacon, also hung around the Slade School. Anyway, I stopped to talk to a slightly strange, plump and large man, who told me he was a sculptor. His name was Eduardo Paolozzi, he lived in London and he was very pretentious.

I didn't know how to tell him that he was ideal for the role of one of the deaf-mutes in my short film. Finally, deeply embarrassed, I asked him if he would play the part, and surprisingly he agreed. Eduardo and Michael, a sculptor and a painter, would end up in the East End playing deaf-mutes who spoke with their hands.

I arranged to meet my friends in the East End at the pub whose owner I had befriended. With me were Eduardo Paolozzi, Michael and Hamad the cameraman. At our leisure, we shot the scenes where the children pester the two protagonists.

It was challenging to explain to the children that they were to approach the two deaf-mutes, insult them, and then run away when the fat one would turn around and try to grab one of them.

The children knew it was pretence, but still were terrified and screamed each time Eduardo would catch one of them - all of which worked perfectly well for me.

My friends too thought that the area, the streets, the channels, and the empty expanses were extraordinary.

It was a cheerful day that ended with us eating curried meatballs in a cheap restaurant we happened upon, managed by an Indian family.

For the interior location of the protagonists' home I found an office next to the river, where I got permission to shoot in two rooms - one that would pass as the dining room and a smaller one that we had to set up as a bedroom.

The next day I went with Michael to Portobello Road to visit the antiques vendor, who had lent us his storage space to shoot K and who had become our good friend.

He gave me plates, a tablecloth, a soup tureen, a nice picture to hang on the wall, and a mirror for the dining room.

For the bedroom he gave me an antique wash basin with a water jug on a tripod stand. I also took some floral wallpaper to decorate the room. All this courtesy of our kind and affectionate antiquarian, David Grisby.

The following day we returned to the pub in the East End, with all the props we needed for our set. We scheduled the next shoot with Eduardo Paolozzi and Hadary the cameraman for the following weekend.

That gave me the time to find a man, a woman and a girl in the neighbourhood who would play the family hosting the two deaf-mutes.

***

Everything was going smoothly, when love suddenly burst into my life. It started when I ran across the legs of an odd fellow whose head was under a 1927 Austin 7, which he was apparently trying to fix.

I was intrigued by the small vintage car and when he came out from under it, dirty and covered in dust, I asked him if he would take me for a ride. He opened his arms as if to offer me all that he owned, which was evidently that little car.

I got in and the car started with a jolt before rolling away. I looked at him as he was driving and I liked him - I really liked him. I liked his profile, his demeanour, his coat, and his hands. How was it possible that I liked everything about him? I laughed with pure joy. He stopped at the end of King's Road in an alley next to the river called World's End. So this is where we came to.

I was terribly excited. He pointed to a little door, where he lived. I was really hoping that he would invite me in and he did, and I happily entered the wolf's den.
He asked me: "What are you doing here in London?" Trying to show off I said: "I'm making a short film".

"Oh, so you're one of those unbearable, tiresome pseudo-artists. I detest foolish women who have opinions."

"I'm not a fool," I answered, deeply offended. "You're a male chauvinist conditioned by a thousand-year old habit of peddling abuse."

He asked me how I, being bird-brained, could ever think of directing a film, and added, by the way, that he was an artist, a real artist, a writer, a poet and also an actor - sufficiently intelligent and lucid to know a fool when he met one. According to him the most foolish women were the ones who had opinions, and he only needed to look at me to know that I was one of those damn women with opinions, one of those royal pains in the arse, one of those sophisticated pseudo-intellectuals, one of those cerebral witches whom he wouldn't have married even if he were paid to do it.

With my face all flushed I screamed at him that to finally have my own opinions I'd had to struggle to get out of the darkness of the Middle Ages, and that I certainly didn't intend to give up this achievement just for the mere pleasure of maybe going to bed with him. How could an artist speak ill of women?

"Oh," he said, wounded in his pride, "perhaps you don't think I'm an artist? Perhaps you'd like to see for yourself all the plays that fill up these drawers?" With a wild expression in his eyes, he pulled out papers and manuscripts from pockets and drawers, and held them under my nose. "This is a tragedy called The King Will Die, and this is a comedy." Beside himself, he waved the papers at me and with a piercing voice yelled that he was an artist, a great artist and that I, being stupid, could never recognise a genius from an ordinary person. "I know perfectly well how to recognise what somebody's worth, since I'm quite out of the ordinary," I said, adding that only an exceptional man could be with an exceptional woman like me. At that point he said that only an exceptional woman could know his worth and be with an exceptional man like him.

So I told him that I didn't underestimate him at all. On the contrary, I considered him an extraordinary person and thought that he hated women because he'd never met an exceptional woman like me, that is, a woman unlike any other. I added that I would be very happy to read or listen to his play The King Will Die. Why do I like men who turn out to despise women?

"You're not homosexual are you?" I asked.

"Why," he replied, "do I look like one?"

I blushed and didn't know what to say.

He leaned over me and kissed me on the cheek. He said he kissed me not because I was a woman but because I was a cat, a kitten that was lost, the kitten he'd always been looking for.

Suddenly I felt the cat side of me taking over and I wasn't able to repress it.

In that moment I felt the beginning of a metamorphosis, whose consequences I couldn't foresee. D said he would recite something for me. He took a cloth from the sofa, donned it like a sort of cloak, and I asked him why he did that. He retreated a few steps and started reciting some verses in a marvellous rhythmic English that I didn't quite understand.

"Did you write this?" I asked. "No," he answered annoyed, "this is Shakespeare!" He moved away again, and recited other verses that had the same rhythm and were as beautiful.

"Shakespeare?" I asked timidly.

"No, these verses are mine."

"They sound beautiful," I said, "but my English isn't good enough."

He turned me inside-out and upside-down. Cat, kitten: where did your claws go? I didn't answer.

I was a cat and I didn't have a voice - the most I could do was purr. Four velvet paws, a pink nose, pink ears, a tiny pink tongue and so much warmth. How could I ever get out of that bed? The bed was large and in the middle of it was a forested valley. The king led his cat, who became more and more cat like, into the valley. Nose to nose, eyes against eyes. He had four eyes, but if I got closer he was left with only one, like a Cyclops. In that bed I felt as wonderful as inside the belly of a whale. I walked inside the whale's belly as I would walk in the belly of the ocean. I stayed put under the covers in warmth and darkness. I didn't want to go out in the fog anymore. He dressed me, combed my hair, brought me coffee in bed, and treated me like his little girl, like his queen. We lived together for a few days.

I spoke about my film and asked him if he would write the dialogue. He wanted to know everything about it, so I explained to him that there were two deaf-mute protagonists, Michael and Eduardo, that we met at the pub in the East End, and that the film's idea was to convey the feeling of being extraneous to society. I told him that I wanted to achieve that effect by suspending all noises and sounds when the camera shot from the point of view of the two deaf-mute protagonists, and resuming the din of normal life when the camera shot the reality in which the two protagonists were immersed.

The leitmotif, the theme of the film, would be the constant switching between the subjective and objective points of view.

D was thrilled, jumped up and said: "I'll get right to work. You go out and get us something to eat". Then he sat in front of his typewriter.

***

When I met my friends at the usual East End pub, I brought D along.

I introduced him to my friends, who were a bit perplexed when he announced that three professional actors were about to join us, to play the family with which the two deaf-mutes were living. As a matter of fact, the previous day, after I'd asked him to take part in the film, D had insisted on finding professional actors to play those roles. In addition, he brought the typed dialogues to give to the actors to memorise.

I hadn't dared say no, persuaded by him to give a "touch of professionalism" to the whole thing. We all moved to the set, in the dining room that Michael and I had decorated for the scene: a table, four chairs, plates and soup tureen, a nice picture on the wall and a mirror.

The three professional actors arrived and D instructed them while the two deaf-mutes, the cameraman and I retreated to a corner waiting to start shooting.

In the scene the two protagonists walked into the room, greeted the husband and wife who were already at the table, and sat down with them. The wife would serve food to everyone, while the daughter announced that she was late and her boyfriend was waiting for her. Looking at herself in the mirror, she would fix her hair.

The scene had to convey their general discomfort, perhaps even their annoyance, before two people who couldn't speak or hear.

While the pretty daughter looked at herself in the mirror, the camera had to catch the young deaf-mute looking at her completely mesmerised.

A delicate world of silence would be interrupted by the noise of the harbour and of the passing ships. The lines had to be: "Please, sit down. Sit. Would you like more? Eat". The words would not be heard by the two deaf-mutes but would be made comprehensible to them by added gestures.

D asked for our complete silence and had the actors read their parts out loud. Then he had them repeat them by heart. Naturally they got their lines wrong, or didn't remember them. They were made to repeat them a third time, and then again. I thought it was going to be just a few lines, but discovered that in D's dialogues the daughter had a boyfriend whom the mother didn't like, who worked as a mechanic, and who made the daughter suffer because he was probably seeing someone else, since a friend of the mother had seen him with another woman...

Then came the father's turn. He brought the discussion back to the food and said that he had to go work at the dock. A friend was waiting for him on a barge under the bridge and he had to help him load because the friend has just been released from the hospital and was not well. Plus the friend's mother was waiting for him and didn't know he wasn't well. At that point the actor had to stand up and walk out of the room.

I realised that I wasn't at all interested in making a film about the life of these people, but wanted to make a film about the discomfort of feeling like an outsider in the world, and I told D.

The cameraman also pointed out to him that he didn't have the equipment to record the images and dialogues in sync, and so the dialogue had to be either cut or dubbed later. D began to act nervously.

I decided to start shooting.

D kept ordering everybody around, and Michael and Eduardo started getting very annoyed. Aware that tragedy was about to strike, I placed the camera in front of the door to film Michael as he walked in. Everyone else was already seated at the table, including Eduardo.

D intervened saying that he thought it best to put the camera behind Michael and see him walk in from the back.

At this point Eduardo stood up and said that he came to act for me and, if that were no longer the case, he and Michael would leave.

Tragedy struck. D ditched me, walking out with his script and telling me he never, ever wanted to see me again.

***

My bed is empty - my love has gone. He's left me, and I almost can't breathe.
I wander around King's Road, stopping in all the pubs to see if he's there, but he isn't. I wander elsewhere, I'm trembling all over, I'm without a master and without a leash. Where's my Daddy? I'm a puppy and I break down in tears.

A fellow stops me and asks: "What's wrong, why are you crying?"

"I'm not crying."

"Let me console you."

"No, thank you."

"Yes, let me walk with you."

I insist: "You're very kind, but no thank you".

He says: "Yes, yes".

I say: "No, no".

"Is it because I'm black?"

"No, no."

"Then let me walk with you, I'll buy you a drink" he said.

"No, no."

"Is it because I'm black?" he insists.

"No, no, no."

"Then come and have a drink with me."

I don't want to offend him and so I have a beer with him. Then he says: "I'll walk you to your place". The more he insists the harder I cry.

Instead of being with my love, I'm with a chap who was pestering me and whom I don't want to offend.

These words come to my mind: *Oisive jeunesse à tout asservie, par délicatesse j'ai perdu ma vie* (Idle youth enslaved to everything, through sensitivity I wasted my life). And so I snap and start to scream.

I watch him walking away despondently into the night, certain of having been rejected because he's black, when instead I'm in love with someone else.

Darkness had fallen all around me.

The solution came to me neatly and clearly - suicide.

Leaving the restaurant where I worked, I'd missed the last underground to go back to my little room, but I didn't want to go back to that horrible room. In fact I didn't want to stay in this city at all, or on this earth, in this world. It was so dark all around me that I just slumped to the pavement and began to sob. I was crying so hard that I barely saw the face of the policeman who bent over me saying: "Come on baby, don't cry". But I kept on crying and sobbing. I felt my body being lifted from the ground and found myself between two policemen who told me: "Come on baby, come with us".

They had me take a seat in their car and drove me away.

I found myself in a small room at the police station, with the two of them going out of their way to console me.

They brought me a cup of tea with milk and sugar and asked me why I was crying so hard. I told them that he'd left me and they told me that he didn't deserve me because you don't leave a pretty girl like me and that I deserved a man who was kind and sweet and understood my ambitions and not a man who wanted to compete with me and made me feel like a fool. When they saw that I'd calmed down they took me into another small room. "Now sleep baby," they said, and they turned off the light and closed the door, wishing me goodnight.

VI

Desperate and alone, I stood in the lab where my angel from the British Film Institute had sent me to edit the film. There was a moviola, and celluloid film scattered everywhere.

When Denis Forman asked me how I was doing, I told him I was "drowning in a sea of celluloid". So he said, "I have three people here making another movie for me. One of them is an extremely bright film critic who is also very gruff, but if he likes what you shot I'm sure he'll help you edit it". That's when Lindsay Anderson appeared, a cranky young man who looked at me diffidently, and said he wasn't sure he could do anything for me. After looking at the footage, however, he told me "all right, I'll help you edit it".

So my angel saved me for a second time, sending me his emissary Lindsay. Lindsay and I became such good friends that I was invited for dinner at his flat nearly every night. Another regular and enthusiastic guest at these dinners was Daniele Paris, my friend who had composed the music for my film K.

When Lindsay saw the film, in fact, he liked the music so much that he asked Daniele to come to London to do the soundtrack for Together.

Lindsay's curried meatballs were an irresistible attraction, and he would preparc them and serve them as though it were a sacred ritual.

Lindsay and I had a curious relationship. He was always bossing everyone around, and I would often respond by saying "Yes, my captain". In him I finally found someone caring who treated me as a kind father would.

Dinner at Lindsay's usually featured curried meat-balls with potatoes and vegetables, followed by whiskey and songs sung on the guitar. Lindsay had such a wonderful voice - when he sang he trans-formed from a bossy lieutenant into a passionate romantic.

Daniele Paris, who in Italy worked as an orchestra conductor and an avant-garde composer, loved the folk songs that Lindsay sang, and chose one of them, a children's tune, for the soundtrack of Together.

Lindsay had a beautiful home, with a large living room that gave onto a small garden. It was a real hub, and whenever we were there for dinner people were always coming and going. Many of them were actors and dancers, because Lindsay was one of the directors at the Royal Court Theatre.

At Lindsay's I met Gavin Lambert, the famous film critic who wrote for Sight and Sound. He was a shy and elusive man, and I could tell they'd been friends for a long time.

Lindsay was also a film critic and had founded the magazine Sequence, where he wrote at length about John Ford, the film director he loved the most because he was, as Lindsay said, all about friendship.

He told me he had gone to the United States to interview John Ford for a last time, and at the end of the interview had asked him if there was anything he could do for him. And John Ford told him: "Just be my friend".

So I asked Lindsay what I could do for him and he smiled and said: "Be my friend". Almost embarrassed by his sentimentality, he immediately added: "Best to have dinner now".

***

One day Daniele announced that he'd finished composing the music for the film. Before our meeting with the musicians, he came in beaming, score in hand.

I was thrilled by the idea that the accompaniment to my film was written on those pieces of paper. Lindsay chose to call the film Together, a title I liked because it highlighted the friendship between the two deaf-mutes.

Friendship was what motivated Lindsay, and I knew that for him a friend was forever.

The three of us sang as we went to the studio, where the sound engineer John Fletcher, a friend of Lindsay's, was waiting for us.

As we walked in, I was surprised to find five musicians waiting for the conductor and ready to play. The lights went down and there was total silence as Daniele stepped on the podium.

Daniele directed them with confidence, and I was struck by how he engaged the musicians with just a few assertive gestures.

I heard the music of the film for the first time, and I liked it.

You could tell that Daniele was completely at ease in his role - in Italy he had a reputation for being, if not the only, one of the few conductors of modern music. When the recording was over Daniele thanked the musicians and we took a break.

"Bravo, that was brilliant," said Lindsay, "now let's have a nice cup of tea". We all welcomed the idea.

Daniele turned to Lindsay: "You know, Lindsay, I was impressed by the civility of these musicians".

"How do you mean?"

"Well, if they'd been Italian, I probably would've had to call their attention several times. It's very difficult to have silence in the hall because they're always chatting and getting distracted, and so I end up blowing a fuse and screaming. This is why I have a reputation for being a cantankerous neurotic".

Lindsay looked at him understandingly and asked: "Would you like to come back and conduct the music for one of my films then?"

"Of course, I'd love to come back".

"It's a deal then!"

"And this is a promise," said Daniele.

We went back to the studio to synchronise the music and add the sound effects - the children's screams and the noises of the harbour.

The very last sound was the siren of a distant ship entering the port, as a barge slowly moved away, and the caption "The End" appeared on the screen.

We had finished the film and were all delighted and moved.

Lindsay turned very serious and said: "I think we deserve to have something to eat". "You're right, we deserve it!"

***

Lindsay asks me to meet him at the British Film Institute because he wants to show me the film he finished shooting, as well as the one made by his friends Tony Richardson and Karel Reisz.

Both impress me, but before I have the time to say anything, Lindsay pulls me along to see his friends at a cafe in Soho. They've seen my film and absolutely want to meet me.

Tony is a young theatre director and Karel works as film officer for the car manufacturer Ford, and this is their first film, financed by the BFI Experimental Film Fund. Karel, Tony and Lindsay all speak in impeccable Oxonian English.

We meet in a very cosy cafe in Soho owned, as I discover, by an Italian. London is filled with pubs, and this is one of the rare cafes. Lindsay looks at me eagerly and said: "Tony, Karel and I find that our films and yours have some things in common, Lorenza. We share a way of looking at the world, an attitude towards others that entails respect and a human solidarity, which are sorely missing today".

Karel intervenes: "We love the importance that you give to ordinary people and everyday life. I think this is the element we have in common".

Tony goes on: "This attitude erases all class divisions and in particular the difference between the somebodies and the nobodies. What I mean to say is that our working-class people feel like nobodies, they've lost all their dignity and just go out and get drunk every night, because they have no say in any matter". Lindsay says that the time had come to put our charming friends and their cockney accent

Still from Lorenza Mazetti's film Together (1956)

on the screen. During the war they didn't feel like nobodies and they weren't treated with contempt because they were needed to fight the Germans.

Tony notes the fact that my characters can't take part in the outside world. For example in my film K, the protagonist Gregor embodies the malaise that is the basis to any real rebellion, and his alienation is, in fact, an indictment against the society around him. Kafka meant the opposite of what he said: Gregor was depicted as the accused, guilty of not fitting into society, when in fact he was the accuser.

The true message of the artist rests on the impact he has upon his audience.

The impact of The Metamorphosis, in fact, is one of indignation towards Gregor's father, who represents society.

"The revolution is borne out of this anguish and alienation," says Karel.

Surely an artist who wants to blame society wouldn't do that directly. For example, in Lindsay's film O Dreamland, the contrast between the song I Believe and the images of a mass of dehumanised people creates an effect of indignation, or so it seems to me.

Shyly, I say that in Tony and Karel's Momma Don't Allow, the two upper class couples walk into the jazz club but can't push themselves to take part in the frenzied dance, as they feel superior to the crowd of wretched people. Their gesture of unscrewing the winged victory from the bonnet of their Rolls Royce for fear it might get stolen is very effective.

Lindsay cuts into the conversation and says: "We are here to write a manifesto, aren't we?"

"Yes, sure."

"Well, let's write it then!"

He takes a few sheets of paper and a pen and starts writing.

"I don't know if you agree, but I think we should call this the Free Cinema Movement."

"Why free?"

"Free cinema in the sense of experimental films. Films that don't aim to make money but to simply be a means of expression for filmmakers, free from restrictions imposed by producers and distributors, by the script or even by the technique. Just as we had the opportunity to express ourselves without obligations and without the aim to make a profit, there must be scores of other young filmmakers around the world who are producing something important with little money. Well, we have a film theatre here that we can use and we could invite to London all these young filmmakers from America, from France, from Poland. We have the opportunity to showcase their films and give them visibility. We have the film critics and the press. London must become a trampoline for young artists who are not known and who deserve to be known. We can organise an international festival of experimental cinema, a festival for the independent films of each country".

"The British Film Institute will give us the possibility of welcoming these artists and to make them known. It will be up to us to give them the glory. Stand up, stand up!"

"At this point, it would be best if you all signed this."

And so we did, enthusiastically.

These films were not made together; nor with the idea of showing them together. But when they came together, we felt they had an attitude in common. Implicit in this attitude is a belief in freedom, in the importance of people and the significance of the everyday.

As filmmakers we believe that:

No film can be too personal.

The image speaks.

Sound amplifies and comments.

Size is irrelevant. Perfection is not an aim.

An attitude means a style.

A style means an attitude.

LORENZA MAZZETTI, LINDSAY ANDER-
SON, KAREL REISZ, TONY RICHARDSON

***

A few days later Karel Reisz invites us for lunch at
his home to discuss things in more detail.

I arrive to find him fully occupied with a shrieking
toddler while his lovely wife is preparing our meal.

Karel is cheerful and entertaining, treating me like
an old friend. Contrary to my expectations, we
don't talk about serious things at all.

At one point Karel frowns and looks at me gravely

I thought he was about to talk to me about some deep philosophical matter or other. He rests a hand on my shoulder and leaning towards me says into my ear: "Lorenza, would you be able to tell me why my son destroys any toy I give him to see what's inside it? Do you think it's normal?"
"Of course it is," I say amused.

The British have a great ability to treat mundane things very seriously and tragic ones very lightly - what one calls understatement.

Once lunch was over we leave in good spirits. The following day, Lindsay takes me to see Tony Richardson at the Royal Court Theatre, the famous theatre in the centre of London. Tony is young and handsome, with a tall slender figure, and like Karel and Lindsay speaks perfect Oxbridge English. He tries to play down his qualities by speaking haltingly, using his shyness as a defence against the envy of others.

After congratulating me he begins a long discussion with Lindsay, which I understand to be about a play to be scheduled.

The next day Lindsay takes me to meet Mr Robinson, the director of the National Film Theatre, who is in charge of programming for the cinema run by the BFI.

He is a dashing gentleman, who reminds me of the actor Trevor Howard.

Lindsay asks him if we could use the film theatre in Waterloo for a week, to screen our films and launch our manifesto.

The director tries to come up with excuses, saying that other films had already been programmed, but Lindsay stares straight into his eyes with the look he uses in crucial moments as if to say: "Don't even think about saying no". He stares at him and says: "This is not a request, it's an order".

Mr Robinson bursts out laughing and says: "Well, since it's an order I can't say no". Lindsay takes me by the arm and says: "Let us go now".

Mr Robinson didn't know that it was only the beginning, and that we would occupy his cinema with screenings of independent films by young directors from France, the United States and other countries again and again!

***

I return to my waitressing job at The Soup Kitchen. I'm starving, and I'm late. As I wait tables I'm in such a state that I can't keep the orders straight. I bring pea soup to a customer who has ordered a tomato soup.

It's late, I'm exhausted and can barely stand on my feet, and when he protests I kindly ask him to accept the soup I've brought him. Annoyed, he says he doesn't want it, and I plead with him not to send it back. I leave him to wait other tables.

Through the corner of my eye I see him get up and walk to the cash desk, where he complains to the manager as he points at me threateningly, before returning to his table. After being reprimanded, I bring him the soup he had ordered and, leaning towards him say: "He's going to fire me, are you happy now?" and walk away. He eats in silence, then gets up and leaves. He's the type of man I detest: attractive, young, and obviously wealthy.

I go on working and at closing time grab my jacket and purse and walk out. It's dark and cold. I see a nice car parked by the curb, with someone inside looking at me. It's the soup fellow. He lowers the window, calls me, and with a desperate look pleads to be forgiven.

It's the last thing I expected. The monster has become human. Touched, I accept his apologies and he asks me if he can drive me home. He works in advertising, and wants to show me his work. He's handsome, rich and kind, but my heart is elsewhere.

***

On the appointed day at five pm the four of us met, all excited, at the National Film Theatre in Waterloo.

Our short films were to be screened one after the other, and Lindsay would stay at the entrance selling copies of the manifesto.

Tony, Karel and I were all fretting, wondering what was going to happen.

We were amazed to see a queue of people lined up for half a mile outside the cinema. How was that possible?

When the screenings ended there was great cheering. The Observer and The Sunday Times wrote of "white hope" for cinema, and Gavin Lambert wrote many flattering things about us. The four of us were invited to appear on a television programme hosted by a very famous man who talked to me condescendingly.

His name was Dimbleby or something.

A pastor in the audience stood up and told me: "The East End children are not as nasty as you depict them".

I tried to explain to him that my film was not a documentary.

After the television appearance we went to a bar and Lindsay said we'd earned a glass of whiskey. We started making fun of each other, laughing and joking.

"How do you think it all went?" Tony Richardson asked a bit anxiously.

"I'd say well," said Karel in his impeccable English. "It went well, except that you were sweating like pig!" said Lindsay in his finest Oxbridge accent. Karel was surprised: "Was I really sweating so horribly?"

"It's not true, it was just that Lindsay's huge nose was shading your face," said Tony.

Lindsay turned to me with a look of surprise: "Lorenza, was I shading him with my nose?"

"Yes, you were shading everyone."

At this point Lindsay turned very, very serious. Was he offended?
He stared at us with one of his killer looks that meant, "You idiots wouldn't dare contradict me, would you?" Then he opened his mouth and said,

"I think the time has come to send the same shock waves through the theatre".

"Yes, you're right," said Karel with an air that made his yes definitive.

"Yes," whispered Tony pensively.

After all, both Lindsay and Tony were directors at the Royal Court Theatre. Lindsay turned to Tony with an inquisitor's tone: "Some time ago you told me you received a script full of abuse. Where did you put it?"

"It must be on some shelf with other papers. I don't know exactly where, but I'll look for it."
"It'd be best if you found it right away."

"I wouldn't want someone to call the police during the performance and shut down the production."

"Who is the abuse directed to?" asked Karel.

"Against the establishment, of course," answered Tony.

Lindsay said: "That's fine, we just need to announce that there'll be a public debate at the end of the performance and that everyone will have a chance to speak".

"We'll be there in the front row," we all agreed. And Lindsay added: "What's the name of the playwright?"

"I don't recall, he's young, I believe his name is Osborne."

"And the title of the play?"

"I can't remember."

A month later the four of us met at the Royal Court Theatre.

Tony went backstage with John Osborne while Lindsay, Karel and I went to sit in the audience ready to give a hand.

During the performance of Look Back in Anger insults were hurled from the stage, and from the house back to the stage. A debate took place at the end of the performance, and it was as though a bomb had gone off.

When I was with my friends I had the impression of being in the company of the three musketeers: Tony Aramis, Karel Athos, and Lindsay d'Artagnan. Everyone was talking and shouting, and I barely understood what they were saying. In any case, the establishment got what it deserved.

The day after the performance of John Osborne's work, we delved into the newspapers. As Lindsay had foreseen, a large part of the establishment press focused mainly on the protagonist, describing him as a neurotic, angry young man that talked a lot of nonsense.

Kenneth Tynan of The Observer, instead, was full of praise for the play. The result, at any rate, was that the theatre was always full at each performance. Boosted by the play's success, we met at Lindsay Anderson's home to draw up our battle plan. "And now, we must storm the Bastille!" said Lindsay bringing to the table his curried meatballs and serving them with religious devotion.

"What do you mean?" asked Karel.

"We've got to take over the National Film Theatre for at least a month and screen independent films made by young filmmakers from around the world, which are just laying there unseen and undistributed."

"Brilliant idea!"
"You take care of that," said Lindsay to Karel.

"All right, I can take care of it."

"Lorenza and I will go to Sight and Sound and talk to Gavin Lambert, who should contact young American independent filmmakers through his friends at Film Culture - Jonas Mekas should come over with his whole crew," said Lindsay giving orders like a colonel before the battle, "and I'll take care of France by calling Louis Marcorelles and getting the people hanging about La Revue du Cinema to come."

"What about me?" said Tony.

"You", answered Lindsay, "have the most difficult and crucial task. We need to be able to make our films on our own, without asking anyone for help, especially those dreadful distributors. I don't want to make a film and then have to cut it all up because they don't want to see a worker's face on the screen."

"I want Britain to be a place where cinema can be respected and understood by everyone. I care about having my films shown to British audiences and I think our working-class friends deserve a place of honour on the screens of their country." Lindsay's face was all flushed. It wasn't clear whether he was perspiring because he'd been shouting or because he'd been cooking.

Tony stood up and said: "Yes, we have to establish our own production company. We'll produce each

Lorenza Mazzetti on the set of Together

other's films. Karel, you'll produce Lindsay's film and I'll produce yours".

This is how Woodfall Film Productions, the company that would produce our films, was created. It took but a few curried meatballs and some whiskey to plan a part of British cinema that went down in history.

***

To follow the screening of our own films, the second Free Cinema programme took place, as part of an ongoing series.

The first to arrive in London were the Americans. I was particularly struck by Lionel Rogosin, a young man with a stunning face who came from a Russian family and had a rabbi grandfather. His father had arrived in America penniless and had made a fortune, which Lionel was now busy squandering. Lionel brought a wonderful film and told us about the movie theatre he'd opened on Bleecker Street in New York City, where he screened independent films that struggled to find a distributor.
His film On the Bowery was about a drunken spree in the neighbourhood that was known to be Manhattan's skid row.

A few minutes into the film, the viewer had the feeling of really being on that street, among destitute people talking and getting drunker by the minute. There was no judgement. It was a fantastic film.

Jonas Mekas arrived surrounded by young girls, in a cloud of smoke. The group emanated an intoxicating scent, and someone whispered in my ear that they were smoking pot. Mekas walked in, bare-foot as was his custom, looking like a guru. His film was entitled Guns of the Trees.

Then came James Broughton with The Pleasure Garden, Stan Brakhage with Anticipation of the Night, Gregory Markopulos, and an extremely lovable Richard Leacock, who billed himself as a documentarian, although you couldn't help laughing at what his eyes captured of reality.

The question was raised: is it possible to document reality without interpreting it in some way, without your eyes choosing to see some aspects of it to the detriment of others? Documenting reality with humour was certainly a very personal thing.

Finally Kenneth Anger arrived with Scorpio Rising, a film in which image and sound switched roles, with the images mostly providing a visual track to the songs. Basically without dialogue, the film focussed on the dressing ritual of a motorcycle gang member before he climbs on his bike. There was something sacred about the ritual of this young man who rode off and died.

Later it would be the turn of John Cassavetes's Shadows, a black and white film whose plot was given to the actors only as an outline within which they could improvise, acting their given role as they chose. The director too had been free to improvise, so that the entire film had a marvellous extemporaneous quality to it, and emotions emerged unexpectedly.

Cinema is really about this, and not about slavishly following a fixed script, as distributors usually demand.

The French group was lead by Jean Rouch as well as Chris Marker, who came with his brilliant La Jetée, and there was also Georges Franju with his Le Sang des Bêtes. We were also expecting Joris Ivens.

**

After a few days Lindsay comes to the restaurant and gives me the news that my film Together has been selected for the Cannes Festival and that I will be going to France to represent the UK.

I say that I can't go alone because I'd be too embarrassed and also have nothing decent to wear. He tells me: "Don't worry, we're all driving down together!" We'd go in a convertible, just as in a dream. Lindsay also gives me an envelope full of money, saying: "This is the money we collected for you with the sale of the Free Cinema Manifesto. You can buy yourself a nice dress…".

I motion to refuse the money, but he gives me one of his looks and says: "This is an order!" Laughing, I reply "Yes, my captain".

***

I'm so happy that when I get back to my little room I don't go to sleep and put on an Elvis record instead. It's so good I have to play it over and over, until I'm so taken by the rock'n' roll rhythm that I start to dance. But there isn't much space in the room, so I dance on top of the table. It's the middle of the night. Completely taken by the music, I don't realise the racket I'm making. Suddenly my room door opens and I see my landlady standing there in her nightdress and housecoat looking at me bewildered and outraged. She says: "This is not really something to do, is it?"

"Not really," I reply.

I jump off the table and stop the record.

She looks around then stares at me as she asks: Where are the pictures that were hanging on the wall?"

I point with my finger under the bed.

"You don't like them?"

I don't reply.

"All right. You must leave this room tomorrow, and put my pictures back where they were."

"Give me at least the time to find another place."

She leaves slamming the door but returns to say: "Put them back where they belong!"

I stay awake until the morning and I'm a bit depressed, but I take the underground to go to work.

I stop at a department store and I fill up my pockets, stashing a jar of apricot jam in the right one and a bar of chocolate in the left one. I'm in dire need of them.

I walk out slowly, believing no one has seen me. After two or three steps outside, I hear someone calling me.

I freeze and feel a hand on my shoulder. A man tells me I've dropped my handkerchief. I'm so grateful that I get carried away, kissing him and hugging him. I leave him standing there a bit bewildered and run off towards the restaurant where I work. I vow never to do it again. No, I will never do it again. Once in the restaurant I go down to the kitchen and eat a piece of chocolate. Peter was looking at me enviously, so I'm forced to give him a piece as well. I put the rest of the bar in my jacket pocket. I feel much better.

I go back upstairs to set the tables and see a very handsome and elegant middle-aged man walking into the restaurant. I hope he will sit at one of my tables.

The man turns to the owner at the cash desk and asks him something.

The owner points right at me.

Oh my God, what did I do?

I think about the chocolate bar and frantically run down to the kitchen.

I take the jam jar and chocolate and throw them in the rubbish.

"What are you doing?" Peter asks me as he tries to rescue what I've thrown away.

I'm paralysed with fear as I wait to be called. The man insists on seeing me, so I climb the stairs shaking, repeating to myself: "Go ahead, look in my pockets, I don't have anything!"

Uncle Robert used to make me write fifty times "I will not tell any lies" - had all his punishments been useless?

The handsome man walks up to me and says:

"Lorenza?"

"Yes, I'm Lorenza," I reply.

He stretches out his hand and introduces himself: "I am Erno Goldfinger, I'm an architect, and your friend Guillaume Chpaltine sent me. He wasn't able to come to London to help you because he's finishing his book, but he's looking forward to your return to Florence. So he sent me to help you. I'm at your disposal, please tell me what I can do for you".

He invites me to his home on Willow Road in Hampstead. "Be there at 12:30" he says walking out.

I ring Lindsay Anderson, telling him that I've moved and I'm staying at 2 Willow Road, where I'm expecting him for lunch.

I can't wait to see his face as he walks into such an amazing house!

The avant-garde architect Erno Goldfinger and his wife Ursula have invited me to stay in their magnificent home.

Ursula has cooked, lunch is ready, I've set the table and Erno goes to open the door for Lindsay. He walks in and his jaw drops. Erno welcomes him and says: "Lorenza is staying with us. We so enjoy being with her that we decided to adopt her, at least until our children come back from the holidays".

Lindsay is astonished as Erno shows him their home - the Leger, Max Ernst and Marcel Duchamp paintings on the walls, the Giacometti sculpture, the photo portrait of Ursula by Man Ray. "We're in full Surrealist mode," he says laughing. Suddenly a wall in the living room opens and disappears, revealing the dining room. Increasingly surprised, Lindsay sits down at the table as another wall opens and Ursula appears, walking towards us from the kitchen with a platter of roast meat. We all sit down at the table.

We speak about Free Cinema, Brecht, theatre and Lindsay's upcoming play at the Royal Court. After lunch we sit in the living room and Erno plays a record of Kurt Weill music. A bit drunk, we all start singing "Mack the Knife" together. After a good time, Lindsay gets up to leave and I kiss him and hug him goodbye. I watch him walk away through the trees, as gusts of fresh spring air make the branches quiver. He turns around and shouts: "We're going to Cannes in a month, don't forget!"

"Yes, my captain!" I reply.

Off he goes in his creased white linen jacket.

I walk back into the house smiling - I have a family waiting for me. It's not the first time I've been adopted.

***

We drive down in a convertible with the wind in our faces - just as in Liala's books.

We arrive in Cannes, a lovely city by the sea, and find a place to stay in the old part of town. From there we go to the Promenade, where the Palais du Festivals appears in all its magnificence.

We run into Cesare Zavattini - the Italian writer and artist whom I admire so much and whose books I have devoured - and Lindsay introduces me to him. Zavattini tells me: "Lorenza, your film apparently received a great deal of praise, but don't tell anyone because it's a secret".

Together won the prize in the Avant-garde category for the UK.

Lindsay and I were so happy, we exchanged a long hug.

In the Festival's daily magazine, Simone Debreuille wrote that Together was a film that needed to be loved tenderly like Jean Vigo's films.

Lindsay and my other friends left for London, while I decided to dash to Florence to see my twin sister Baby.

VII

Baby was waiting for me with open arms. Her husband had left to teach at a university in the United States while she stayed behind in Florence with her young daughter. I found her with a new partner named Vincenzo.

Baby cuddled me and mothered me - she was the one person in the world who really understood me. Chirping like a nightingale, she would talk to me for hours, and from the sweet tone of her voice I picked out key words such as: Brava! Don't worry. It's not important. You'll see - everything will work itself out. I'm here with you. I'll never leave you.

She tucked me under the covers and I fell asleep to the sounds of the countryside of my childhood.

Baby and I are running towards voices that are calling us. How wonderful to hear our names echo in the woods. Here we are! Our parents are already sitting at the dining table, and so are Cicci and Luce.

We are like the rebel twins in The Captain and the Kids, always getting in trouble. We break glasses, we walk through freshly sown fields, we tell lies. After washing our hands, we climb onto our chairs and start eating our pasta. Before our gigantic parents, Baby and I are so tiny, like Hans and Fritz.

"Where have you been? I told you not to wander away from the villa."

We got lost in the woods.

"I told you not to go into the woods."

"Yes, but the tiny golden ball fell to the bottom of the well, so Mr Frog went to fetch it. In return, he now wants to eat out of our little plate, drink from our teeny glass and sleep in our tiny bed."

Baby takes out of her pocket a small bright green frog that leaps onto the dining table. Our uncle stands up annoyed.

Leaning towards Aunt Nina's ear he whispers to her in German - he always talks to her in German when he's angry - that we are to write fifty times "You do not put frogs on the table".

Baby hugged me and tied a colourful bead necklace around my neck. "It looks so good on you," she said, "you should always wear one." She combed my hair, changed my hairstyle and asked her new psychoanalyst friend: "How does she look?"

He nodded in approval, holding Baby's daughter in his arms because Baby was too busy making me beautiful, putting rouge on my cheeks and changing my clothes. As a matter of fact, my trousers were filthy, and I also hadn't changed my socks, which were sticking to my feet. I was terrified of water and didn't want to bathe, afraid that the water would wash away what little life was left in me. Yet Baby and her new boyfriend decided that a hot bath was what I needed, so while Baby made dinner and he took care of her baby, entertaining her with funny voices, I soaked in the hot water and floated. It was summer, there were crickets chirping, there was grass and leafy trees...

Baby put me to bed and kissed me goodnight. Baby enters the room dancing, wearing Luce's best dress which is too big for her. She looks at herself in the large gilded mirror. "What are you

doing Baby, why are you wearing Luce's dress?"
Baby looks at me smiling as her red stains appear
on her dress. On her forehead are two tiny holes
from which blood gushes out, dripping over her
dress, her eyes, her neck, her legs, her feet, and
onto the floor. A burst of submachine gun fire
shatters the mirror. More shots, screams and the
sound of booted footsteps echo inside the house.
Baby lies on the floor in a pool of blood.

I look at her closely and Baby is no longer Baby,
she is Luce. Next to her Uncle Robert, Aunt Nina
and Cicci, lie on the floor lifeless.

Glass windows shatter, mirrors tremble and chan-
deliers sway. I scream, and Uncle Robert stands up
covered in blood, smiling at me. I run down the
staircase calling Baby and as I turn around I see
Luce advancing with holes in her head, looking at
me and smiling. She's coming towards me and says
something, but the yelling of the soldiers is much
louder than her voice.
"Nanny, tell us a story." "What kind of story?"
"The story of the fairy godmother." "No, because
you're not good little girls." "Come on nanny tell
it to us, tell us the story of the fairy godmother."

"Be quiet, be quiet, and don't make any noise.
Here comes your uncle. Uncle Robert? He is
gone, he is dead, he took his life, and he went to
heaven."

Lorenza Mazetti

Elsa begins to sing the Ave Maria. Her voice is high. It fills the heavens and it fills our home. Our nanny sings and can't stop. She speaks of God and of the blessed souls up in the sky and of all those who are up there, in the glory of God. She recites the Apostles' Creed to us and tells us about the resurrections of bodies. The graves break open and everyone is resurrected - this is what she says. Her voice fills up the entire house. Baby and I are under her shawl, resting on her knees while all the others are up in heaven. The nanny sings and her bosom lifts and drops. Her voice is like the voice of an angel, filling my ears with extraordinary images. The sound of her voice fills the house, and outside the Lungarno flows with the river. Elsa, Baby and I are here on earth and all the others are in heaven. Darkness creeps up on us like this, the three of us hugging as the curtains flutter. In the darkness I can hardly see the large fireplace and our uncle's library.

The soldiers came in through the open doors. God is an empty atrium resounding with their booted footsteps. How can it be that our dead never show up? That they remain underground when their shoes are still next door in the entrance hall?

In my heavenly kingdom there won't be a Kingdom of Heaven. I might upset Elsa, but I can't even bring one God into my bed. I look at the Christ at the head of my bed and think that I'll marry a man who looks like him.

Baby says: "God exists if you believe in him, otherwise he doesn't".

And so our dog Ali crawled on top of me and put a paw on my chest. I told him to go away because he was soiling my dress, but he wouldn't leave. Then Ali turned into a wolf that wanted to devour me, so I became very frightened and called out for Baby, who turned on the light and told me not to worry because Ali wasn't there. He too had been shot dead, along with Cicci and Luce and Aunt Nina, and then Uncle Robert as well. Baby kissed me and hugged me.

I fell back asleep, and Uncle Robert was telling me that I had nothing to fear, he said "don't worry" and just kept on smiling. Yet I couldn't help worrying and had to turn on the light. I kept my eyes wide open because I didn't want to fall asleep, and felt slumber filling me like water filling a jug. The water came up to my mouth and then it reached my eyes and my eyes floated in sleep like jellyfish. I didn't want to sleep.

I got up, and wandered around the house.

Baby came looking for me in the middle of the night. She and Elsa brought me back to bed.

***

I knew it was sad for someone not to believe in God anymore, especially for someone like me, who used to really believe in him. To tell the truth, when I was a child I loved God, Jesus and Il Duce as well. I loved them all in the same way I loved Uncle Robert, except that I loved Jesus a bit more than God, and God a little less than Il Duce.

When Elsa dragged me to church in Piazza Santa Croce I looked at that crucified Christ and at the red blood dripping from his ribs, feet and hands, and it reminded me of them and of the blood on their faces and on their clothes. I would start screaming that it wasn't fair, it wasn't fair that people got killed just like that, simply because their father was a Jew. What was it with that curse? Weren't Jews supposed to be God's chosen people?

Elsa got cross and said: "Miss Penny, you're awfully confused, in just a few months you have gone from one religion to the next, and are going around in circles. You start railing against priests and against God himself and then become a Protestant. God forbid, you filled our ears with this Martin Luther, this complete rascal...".

"For your information, Elsa, Luther was not a rascal. And the Buddha too was a great man."

"Since your mouth is open, why don't you put some spaghetti inside it, or is the food not to your liking? Look at Miss Baby, she's already finished her plate."

During the daytime I would take the lead, but at night Elsa was hard as a rock, she grew as fast as grass, filling the house and threatening my fragile foundations. At night, Elsa was no longer Elsa. She was in her bed with God in her arms.

Instead, lying in the darkness, I only held fragments of thoughts. Pieces of memories, a firefly, a Beethoven sonata and the Wehrmacht in my bed.

***

Lucian Freud

Dennis Forman

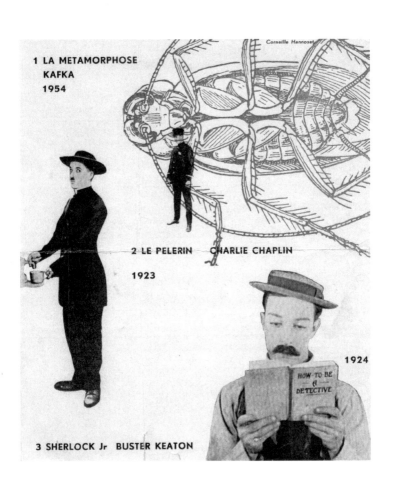

Corneille Hannoset

1 LA METAMORPHOSE
KAFKA
1954

2 LE PELERIN   CHARLIE CHAPLIN
1923

1924

HOW TO BE
A
DETECTIVE

3 SHERLOCK Jr   BUSTER KEATON

Poster for Metamorphosis

Every Sunday we would go to the cemetery. It took no time for the weeds to cover the stone. We are above the ground, we are below the ground. The girls with dirt in their eyes, our uncle with dirt in his eyes sailing under the ground because he was a Jew. A wall of water broke over me like an enormous wave. "Don't cry" said Baby leaning over me and giving me a kiss. We went back home. Elsa put cold compresses on my burning forehead.

The doctor bent over me putting the stethoscope on my heart. He looked at me bewildered. Save me, I whispered in his ear. Surely he must've recognised my illness, but he acted as if nothing had happened. Baby is on the tree branch. It's summer and we are picking figs. Baby is four years old. Baby is in primary school, Baby is growing - the sunflower field, the wheat. Baby is taller than the wheat. Baby's red coat is too short. Baby is growing, and so am I. Glossy rain boots, cyclamens in the woods. We pick wild strawberries, we pick our dreams. Baby in my bed, my poems. Who will I read my poems to now? Baby doesn't love me anymore.

"Who is that pretty boy?"

"He's a foreign student who is here on a scholarship. His name is Stephen". Baby has changed, she struts around in her dress, adorns herself with necklaces and bracelets.

Baby brushes away her unruly curls from her forehead. As I watch her from behind a curtain my heart begins to shrink. Eventually it will disappear, leaving in its place only a crystal.

Baby flutters around the house like a butterfly then walks down the stairway holding her small purse and dives into Stephen's arms. My heart stops beating.

Baby has changed. How many times has she gone out with that playboy? The house is empty without her.

I'm reeling. Baby is with Stephen. What shall I do? Baby went with Stephen. Baby is mine, I scream: "Let her go!"

"No, I'm not letting her go" says Stephen.

"Baby is mine" I scream, grabbing Baby by the arm and pushing Stephen away. "What are you doing, Penny?"

With her cheeks flushed Baby bends over Stephen who has fallen on the floor.

"Don't hurt Stephen!" Baby yells, her cheeks on fire.

Stephen shoves me away. He takes Baby by her arm and pulls her away.

I jump on her.

"Come with me!"

"No! Come with me" he shouts.

I hold on to Baby with all my strength.

"Let me go" says Baby, wriggling out of my hold. I grab her once again.

"Let me go" she says breaking free.

"I hate you" I scream, as the two descend the stairway.

I stand at the top of the stairs.

"Go, go with Stephen" I yell, "I hate you, I hate you".

"I hate you!"

I fly down the stairs and catch up with Baby. I grab her hand and yank her away from Stephen.

"If you want your sister you'll have to marry her" yells Stephen as he takes Baby back and leads her towards the door, acting as if he owned her.

"Why? Do you think you're marrying her?" I scream.

"Sure we're getting married, aren't we Baby?" he says as he pulls her close.

Baby turns around and says: "Yes, we're getting married!"

I barely manage to get hold of Baby's arm again, and I pull it forcefully. Along with Baby, I'm pulling the whole house, my whole past through that crack in the door. I am tugging one way, Stephen is tugging the other, somebody yanks, somebody screams. Baby's finger crushed in the door. Who hurt Baby?

I didn't hurt Baby.

No! Stephen is the one who closed the door.

Baby screams in pain.

How could I hurt my little twin sister? I run away.

I hurt Baby.

***

I want to go away, get on the first train, leave this city immediately.

First, however, I have to go to the bathroom.

I'm told that the toilets are below the station.

I go down the stairs and a policeman tells me to go straight and to the right. All the toilets in Italy are straight and to the right.

The policeman has a gun. Maybe I should go to Germany and kill the people who murdered my relatives. Yes, that's what I should do, but how to steal the gun, or where to find another one and, moreover, who are the murderers? Who gave them the order to kill? Where can I find them? In which German city are they? The important thing is to board a train and leave, but first I want to have a cup of tea at the bar of the railway station. There are a lot of people, and I sit down but then feel completely lost and feel like crying. I'm leaving now. I'm about to leave.

A tall and lanky young man appears before me, with a beard and long hair that make him look like Jesus.

"Why are you crying?"

Through the tears I open up, telling him everything, flooding him with words. He listens keenly interested, probably understanding nothing of what I'm saying. In his awful Italian he tells me that he's American and that he never wants to leave Florence, this marvellous city. He sits down at my table.

I like him, he's sweet and he writes poetry. I will bring this Christ home with me so that I won't be alone anymore.

We walk around the city holding hands and singing a song whose refrain is "I've got you under my skin...".

We laugh, we hold hands.

Through Milton's eyes I see Florence from the hilltop of Fiesole and I realise that I'm looking at paradise on earth. How could I ever have thought of leaving this city? Everything about it is stunning. We see each other again, spending the evenings with his friends Jack, an American, and a Frenchman named Guillaume. We stroll along the streets and alleys of Florence. We stop in San Frediano, where Guillaume sings songs strumming the guitar. The moon is out, and everything is lovely. The city isn't just any city. It's my home, my beautiful home. I will never leave it. We move to San Lorenzo, and sit on the steps of the church talking, drinking and singing songs until dawn. With such a beautiful moon in the sky how could we go home to sleep?

Walking back from Fiesole one evening we stop at Santa Maria Novella. I want to grab a sandwich at the bar but Milton says he'll take me to the Grand Hotel Baglioni - a friend of his is staying there and he'll certainly offer us something.

He says his friend is a former military intelligence officer who became rich and famous by writing a book on allied-occupied Naples, entitled The Gallery after the city's Galleria Umberto I.

We walk into the hotel and Milton introduces me to the writer whose name is John Horne Burns. A good-looking man with blue eyes and an interesting face, he is sitting on a large sofa surrounded by friends. A couple of black friends are playing jazz, one on piano and the other on trumpet. Everyone is drinking. Mr John Horne Burns is buying drinks for everyone, including the two of us. Sitting on the large sofa of the hotel, he goes on talking while everyone mostly listens and laughs, but I hardly understand anything of what is being said because I don't know English very well. I only see that they are drinking whiskey and are all a bit drunk. I decide to invite them all to my house, taking advantage of the fact that the nanny isn't there, she's gone to the cemetery as usual, while

Baby and I didn't. "I guess I'll be the one to go see the Master's grave and bring him flowers" Elsa said, making me feel guilty.

To Baby's and Stephen's great surprise I arrive home with this group of people.

Burns sits in our uncle's large armchair and continues to dominate the conversation and offer whiskey to everyone. The group brought with them many cans of beer and as they eat sandwiches they toss several cans on the floor.

We had lit candles everywhere and a curtain catches on fire, but we immediately put out the flames. The floor is filthy. Fortunately the nanny isn't here.

Two people are on the carpet kissing, and one is playing our uncle's grand piano. Everyone's smoking and drinking. John Horne Burns goes on talking and pontificating. I can tell he is railing against the Americans and then railing against the whole world. Finally he begins to drawl, his voice becoming hoarse and louder.

He keeps turning to Milton, slapping him on the back and saying "Let's have a drink".

It gets to the point that no one is laughing anymore. Burns turns apocalyptic, declaring that our society is on the verge of collapse, that we're all on a boat about to shipwreck, that we're all about to drown. He frightens me and depresses me - all of us about to drown.

He turns to Milton, saying "You too will return to the States," and Milton says "No, I'm not going back, I want to stay here forever and write poetry". Burns grabs his arm and tells him: "I'm rich and famous, I can afford it but you, you want to be a poet? If you don't want to go back to the States how're you going to eat, how're you going to survive here?" Then he adds: "For now there's my money, right?" and draws Milton close to him. "Get out," says Milton, "get out, get out! I don't want to see you anymore!"

In a fit of anger Burns stands up reeling and screams "Okay, okay! I'm going. I'm going!" He leaves dragging his friends along. Milton stays behind and hugs me tight.

It's late. Baby and Stephen go upstairs to their room.

Milton and I stay below in the living room lying on the carpet, shrouded in a cocoon of shyness. There's a full moon, and we hold each other close. Milton caresses me and like seashells my ears echo the sea.

His caresses come and go like waves, and with each one of them my heartbeat bounces against my ribs. It's a deep night, one in which anything could happen. He kisses me on the lips, leaving two diamonds on the corners of my mouth. With his fingers he gives me breasts of mother of pearl. Desire is pulsing inside my ears.

My body transforms into pure sound and then into feathers, which flutter gently around the room. l am a nest where Milton falls asleep.

I wake up in his arms. Someone outside the window is yelling and calling for Milton. Who is calling my love?

I get up and look outside along the Lungarno delle Grazie, and see the writer, smashed, holding a bottle in his hand, looking up at our window and screaming. He's rambling and calling for Milton. Milton walks up next to me and we both look down at John Horne Burns as he yells.

Everything happens in a flash. Burns is shouting at the top of his lungs, calling Milton and saying that if he doesn't come down he'll jump into the river. He scrambles up onto the parapet next to the river and stands there swaying dangerously on one foot and then the other, screaming and taking swigs from his bottle.

"C'mon Milton, come down!"

Baby and Stephen also come downstairs to watch. He's completely insane. He's capable of anything can't you see? So Milton goes outside to the street.

I see them walk away slowly, Milton struggling to hold up Burns, dragging him back to his hotel. "What's Milton doing with that homosexual?" says Stephen.

I look at him astonished. I turn around and see our nanny dressed in black, back from the cemetery. She looks at the chaos in the room and stares at me reproachfully.

***

I heard Baby's voice calling me, she called my name and yelled: "Come, lunch is ready, we're already at the table".

I got out of bed and went downstairs in my nightgown. I walked into the dining room next to the living room and saw Baby placing a serving bowl on the table and Vincenzo holding the baby.

"How are you feeling?" Baby asked embracing me. "Is the fever gone? Are you feeling better?"

"Yes, I feel better."

"I made spaghetti, chicken and a salad. Sit down." I sat down. How wonderful it was to be embraced, cuddled and nourished.

I sat at the table and looked at the food on my plate.

I was paralysed.

"Eat. Why aren't you eating?" Vincenzo asked. I didn't answer. I looked at the plate, at the fork and knife.

"Why aren't you eating?" asked Baby.

"I can't. The fork pierces my throat and the knife stabs my stomach."

They looked at me astounded.

He bent towards Baby's ear and whispered: "We have to send her to a psychiatrist".

VIII

I stood in front of the door and my hand was shaking as I rang the bell. I tried to imagine what the psychiatrist would look like. I was expecting an older man with grey hair, a typical intellectual wearing glasses, who would look at me compassionately.

I was stunned when a red haired and red bearded giant opened the door and looked down inquiringly at me with his blue eyes, saying: "Good morning".

He led me into a large room filled with books, many of them open on different tables.

He said to me point blank: "Now sit down and write what you want from me on this piece of paper. I'll be back in five minutes".

When he came back he read out loud what I'd written: "Help me not to commit suicide". Unconcerned, he told me with a no-nonsense tone: "All right, let's take care of the problem right away. I believe you must have very good reasons to want to take this step and I won't stop you if you feel the need to do so. There's an open window over there, so please...". He sat down as he pointed at the window.

I didn't jump but smiled, amused and quite taken with him and his attitude. I was ready to do whatever he asked, but what he asked me next proved not easy:

"Tell me what you feel, what you feel in this moment".

I answered: "I think that...".

He interrupted me: "I don't want to know what you think, but what you feel. What are you feeling in this moment?"

"I think you think that maybe I'm..."

"I don't want to know what you think I'm thinking. I've asked you what you're feeling, not what you're thinking. Clearly you don't have the courage to examine your emotions."

From that moment we worked on creative imagination.

He would say: "You're at the seashore and are walking towards the water. How is the sea? How is the sun? What time is it?"

I happily entered the fantasy, with the aim of learning to experience my feelings and emotions. We agreed I would see him once a week.

***

One day I walked into his study and heard music in the background, and asked him to please turn it off. "Why should I turn it off?" he said.

"It bothers me."

"But it's so beautiful!"

"It bothers me. Turn it off, please."

"That's interesting," he said, "very interesting. You don't want to hear this music?"

"I can't stand this music."

"You can't stand Beethoven. Not even Mozart?"

"No, I really can't."

"Who used to play this music? Your uncle or your aunt?"

"Both of them did. They often played piano four hands."

"Are you scared of this music?"

"No, I don't like it."

"You don't want to cry."

"No, it's not true, it's just that it bothers me."

"You're scared of drowning in your own tears, aren't you?"

"Will you just turn it off, please!" I screamed. He got up and raised the volume. The music got louder and louder and despite all my efforts, I couldn't move, I was paralysed - the music was too loud. Towering over me, he looked straight into my eyes and said:

"Now I'm your uncle, I've come here to see you. I'm your uncle, tell me what you've always wanted to say to me but haven't said to me yet. Come on, tell me what you want to say to me!"

The music took over me as he insisted: "Tell me what you've always wanted to say to me but haven't said to me yet".

As an uncontainable sob rose inside me, I whispered: "Uncle Robert, I love you!" and collapsed at his feet in a sea of tears.

I sank to the bottom and as I descended, saw rising to the surface a German soldier toting a sub-machine gun. He pointed the gun at me and fired.

***

They'd been in my unconscious for too long. I couldn't face the memory of that dreadful scene and the unbearable void of their absence. Aunt Nina, my beloved adoptive mother, had hidden under a blanket of oblivion so as not to remind me that she was gone. The void was so terrifying that I couldn't breathe. I no longer felt my heartbeat - but then every once in a while it would come back.

I'm standing with my feet in the grass and there are so many daisies it's impossible not to step on them. Baby, Cicci, Luce and I are trailing her; she is carrying a basket, and we are filling it. The sun is shining, the leaves on the trees are quivering in the breeze and I'm happy. Then I stop to think: I'm happy because she's with us. So I ask myself: what if she wasn't? She is the sun, and without her it would be total darkness. Frightened, I run after her and offer her my flowers. She bends down, smiles at me and gives me a hug. I'm filled with joy and latch on to her, squeeze her tight, hold on to her dress. I won't let her go and burst out crying.

Yes, now I was ready. The time had come. I wanted to talk about them and tell the world what I'd witnessed.

***

I took the train to meet my friend Guillaume, a French author who invited me to stay in his cottage in Sperlonga, a small town perched over the sea, where I was going to write about my childhood.

I sat next to the window in the same train compartment with a priest who was reading his breviary intently. I asked myself if I believed in God and in the afterlife. Then I wondered where they were. Why didn't they get in touch with me somehow?

Did I have faith? Sure, it was nice to go to our church, where there were statues of the saints you could touch and pray to, and where the parish priest wore lace and was helped by Zeffirino, the altar boy.

The church was filled with peasants. The men took off their hats and the women covered their heads with veils. The priest got up and down from the altar, addressing us in an unintelligible language. He spoke in Latin. He stepped down and enveloped us in scented smoke. He was very busy. He moved objects around and took a golden cup in his hands. He uttered more incomprehensible phrases then rang a little bell. Everyone stood up and silence fell inside the church as they all prepared to receive the presence of our Lord Jesus Christ. Children couldn't receive Communion - they had to study catechism first.

Under a tree the children talked about God and Jesus. Sitting on the grass we chatted and joked. Baby warned us that if we chit-chatted, joked and made noise, Jesus wouldn't be able to come to us. So we fell silent. We were all silent for a while, and Jesus came to us. We knew because the leaves on the tree quivered as he passed.

During the journey the priest stopped reading, looked at me and got up. He stands right in front of me and says: "Come on, tell me what faith is". I answer automatically: "Faith is the supernatural virtue by which we believe, based on the authority of God, the truths revealed to us and taught to us by the Holy Catholic Church".

"Good," says the priest, "I can tell you studied catechism. And tell me, how many deadly sins are there?"

"The deadly sins are: sloth, greed, lust, gluttony..."

"You don't know, huh? How many types of sin are there?"

I said: "Twenty, father, there are twenty types!"

"No!" he shouted with irritation. "There are two types of sin, only two: original sin and actual sin. And, tell me, in how many ways does one commit actual sin?" "Actual sin is committed by thoughts, actions and commissions..."

"No! Omissions, not commissions! And now tell me, there is one person who never sins. Do you know who that person is? The... the... the..."

"The father!"

"No! The Pope. And who is the Pope?"

"The Pope is the successor of St. Peter and the visible head of the Church, while Jesus is the invisible head of the Church."

"Good! And how many mysteries of faith are there?"

"The mysteries of faith are five: the father, the unity, the trinity, the incarnation, passion and death of our Lord Jesus Christ."

"No!" screams the priest. "The mysteries of faith are two: Unity and Trinity - and that's one. Incarnation, Passion, death and Resurrection of our Lord Jesus Christ - and that's two. And how many precepts of the Church are there?"

"The precepts of the Church are five," I say, "and they are: hear Mass on Sundays, don't eat meat on Fridays, confess at least once a year and commiserate at Easter".

"No! Communicate at Easter!"

Increasingly distressed, the priest looks around searching for someone who is better prepared than me. "Who can recite the Act of Contrition?" "Me! Me! Me..." I shout excitedly: "Oh my God, I am heartily sorry for having offended you, and I detest all my sins, because of your just punishments, but most of all because they offend you, my God, who are all-good and deserving of all my love…"

"Enough. Good, I can see you studied. All of you remember that if you don't study catechism I won't give you Communion. Let's see, who are the three persons in the Trinity?"

Baby answers: "The father, the mother and the son!"

"And what about God?" the priest asks.

"God is the grandfather."

"Zeffirino, you answer. Who are the three persons in the Trinity?"

"They are: the father of God, the mother of God and the Son of God."

"Oh for Heaven's sake. All right, let me see… Let's change subject. Who killed Jesus?"

"The Jews!" all the children answer in unison.

"Good! And because of this they are de… de… de…"

"Delinquents!"

"No! De... de... de...? You don't know? They are deicides! Because by killing Jesus, they killed God."

And I say: "But my uncle wasn't alive then!"

"It's true, but the blame falls on the Jews forever."

I am dumbfounded, and think that the world's hatred against the Jews, their demonization, transformed the people chosen by God into the people cursed by God, so that their massacre somehow seemed fair and justified.

The priest stands in front of me with his face all flushed, and suddenly lifts his arm and slaps me across the face.

The train stopped. I was getting off. The priest smiled and said goodbye.

My friend Guillaume Chpaltine came to pick me up. I got off the train and ran into his arms. We climbed into his car and drove towards the sea and the small town of Sperlonga.

At home the local farmer woman was waiting for us with a delicious frittata and wonderful pan roasted artichokes. I felt so happy. I would write my book while Guillaume wrote his.

Sitting at the Bar Corallo, in front of Tiberius's grotto and a calm sea, I looked at the blank page unable to tackle it. Finally I plunged into my childhood memories and wrote:

Theme: Give an account of what you have done today.

Development: Today in school the Duce spoke to us and told us to do our gymnastics so as to grow strong, well-behaved and ready in case he should call upon us to defend our great Italy, because there is a war.

I wonder if it's all right for me to love my sister Baby more than the Duce. Because I love Baby the same as Jesus. Just the same as Jesus, and I love Jesus a little more than God, and God the same as Mussolini, and Italy and the Motherland less than God but more than my yellow teddy bear." After writing these lines I took the piece of paper and threw it in the wastebasket - it wasn't appropriate to speak of such an immense tragedy like this, as though I were a little girl.

Fortunately my friend Guillaume, who was writing his book for the publisher Julliard, retrieved the crumpled paper from the basket, read it and said:

"*C'est magnifique!* Continue like this for the entire book!"

"But it's not serious."

"And that is its beauty. You're not writing an essay on Nazism, are you?"

***

Sitting at the Bar Corallo and looking at the sea, I wrote the book in twenty days. I sent it to many publishers, but no one answered me.

After several months and many solicitations, all of them wrote back saying that their publishing house wasn't interested in the manuscript.

I was very sad. However, among the letters was one from Cesare Zavattini telling me that he was enthusiastic about the book and had given it to Attilio Bertolucci, the editorial director of Garzanti. Bertolucci published it immediately and sent it to the Viareggio Prize.

Out of the blue, a young journalist appeared at the door asking for me. He'd been sent by Zavattini. I was invited to the Free Cinema Festival in Porretta Terme, where my films would be screened. Lindsay Anderson would be there as well.

We drove off to Porretta Terme: myself, Guillaume and Bruno Grieco (that was the journalist's name).

I didn't know then that from that moment on I would never leave his side.

Post - Scriptum

Cielo cade (The Sky Falls) was rejected by all publishers at first, however Cesare Zavattini loved it and it gave to Garzanti's editorial director, Attilio Bertolucci, to read. Garzanti then published the book with a preface by Zavattini, and Bertolucci decided to submit it to the Viareggio Prize.

In 1962 The Sky Falls won the Viareggio First Novel Award.

Thirty years later Sellerio republished it as an autobiography with a dedication to Robert Einstein and his family.

A film scripted by Suso Cecchi d'Amico, directed by the Frazzi brothers and produced by Silvia d'Amico was drawn from the book and released in 2000.

In 2010 I depicted life at the villa owned by the Einstein family and by my relatives in eighty paintings. The text for the show's catalogue was naive and amusing, along the lines of The Sky Falls.

The show garnered a great deal of interest from schools and from various Italian municipalities, becoming an itinerant show, held in Rome at the monumental complex of San Michele, in Bologna during the Festival of Porretta Terme, in Florence at the Medici Riccardi Palace, in Mantova at the Casa del Rigoletto, and in other cities in Italy and abroad.

The tragedy of the Einstein family has been censored all these years and is still censored today. The murder of my relatives was bracketed with the many military operations carried out during the wartime period, but I believe it was the execution of a precise order against Einstein's relatives. Indeed, my sister and I, as well as other relatives and all the farmhands living on the property, were spared.

During the negotiations with the Germans on the terms of surrender, the Americans and the British had precise orders to thwart Albert Einstein's attempt to shed light on the massacre of his cousin Robert's family. Presumably they didn't want to bring to trial Kesselring, who was involved in the negotiations and who was freed shortly after the end of the war.

A letter written by Maj. Milton R. Wexler from Fifth Army Headquarters, Office of the Inspector General, to Albert Einstein clearly attests to this, ending with the phrase: "I regret that censorship does not permit me to dwell upon this tragedy which is well known to me...".

Cinema experts began to take an interest in me as a filmmaker, and my two films K and Together emerged as cult movies. A month after the great success of our films' screening, Tony Richardson decided to stage John Osborne's play Look Back in Anger, a script he'd had in his drawer for some time. The play was a sensation. John Osborne's character was described by the press as "an angry young man," an epithet that stuck, and was subsequently used quite often to describe the protagonists of Free Cinema films.

Once the anger had moved from the cinema screen to the theatre, London was ready for something stronger, for great films that were no longer documentary in nature and portrayed the lives of ordinary people in new ways. Karel Reisz and Tony Richardson started producing their own films and those of their film-making friends. Among their numerous and unforgettable early black and white productions was Richardson's A Taste of Honey, the story of a homosexual coming to the rescue of a working-class teenager who has an abusive and drink-sodden mother and who finds out she's pregnant.

The kitchen-sink realism themes were new and interesting, but the actors in these films were also a real discovery: Rita Tushingham in Tony Richardson's A Taste of Honey, Albert Finney in Karel

Reisz's Saturday Night and Sunday Morning, as well as Richard Harris and Tom Courtenay, and finally Malcolm McDowell, the absolute protagonist of Lindsay Anderson's If..., a film that became an icon of British 1960s counterculture.

Anger was not restricted to cinema and theatre, being expressed by novelists such as David Storey and Alan Sillitoe, and philosophers and essayists such as Colin Wilson, whose The Outsider linked back to Albert Camus's The Stranger. The best part of the Free cinema movement, however, was its impact. Young people who would meet in basements to play rock'n' roll came out of their holes like "beetles", as there finally was an influential group that applauded them and recognised their right to express themselves. Thanks to the movement, their voices and songs came out in the open and made history. The Free Cinema movement gave a voice to those who didn't have one, acknowledging their talent and their revolutionary power.

Through the movement he founded, Lindsay Anderson launched the first international festival that showcased films made outside the confines of the industry. To think of the Free Cinema movement as focusing exclusively on issues of the British working class and on the fight against the upper class is reductive, as all the films that came from the United States, Canada, France, Poland,

and other countries were quite varied and had other novel and original themes. London's international festival of independent cinema predated any similar event organised in the context of the French Nouvelle Vague or of American independent cinema, and launched many film directors whose influence on filmmaking is still tangible today.

On 15 March 2013 I was invited to London by the Slade School of Fine Art for a special screening of my films K - the short based on Kafka's The Metamorphosis, which no one there had seen before, and Together.

During this London visit I went to look for the house of architect Erno Goldfinger, where I'd stayed as a guest for some time. To my surprise I didn't find any of his family members living there but a queue of people waiting to visit what had become a small museum, exhibiting the house itself and Goldfinger's art collection.

While writing this book, I discovered that John Horne Burns had died just a few months after I'd seen him in Florence. I hadn't known. Witnesses said he simply "drank himself to death". He was 36 years old.

Just as I finished writing this book, I received a call from Prague, inviting me to take part in a documentary about Karel Reisz, my dear friend who died in 2002. This is how I found out that Karel was one of the many children rescued by Sir Nicholas Winton in the operation known as "Kindertransport", thanks to which he found refuge in England and escaped the death that befell the rest of his family.

I deeply regret not knowing that Karel was Jewish and not opening up to anyone about my childhood. This is the mystery of survivors: first they need to forget in order to survive, and then, as time goes by, they are overcome by guilt for having forgotten and thus not having borne witness to the horror.

This is what I wanted to relate in this London Diary.